Grand Avenue

THE RENAISSANCE OF AN URBAN STREET

by

Biloine Whiting Young
and
David Lanegran

NORTH STAR PRESS OF ST. CLOUD, INC.

Library of Congress Cataloging-in-Publication Data

Young, Biloine, 1926-
        Grand avenue : the renaissance of an urban street / by
Biloine Young and David Lanegran.
        224 p. 253cm.
        ISBN 0-87839-105-3 (alk. paper)
        1. Grand Avenue (Saint Paul, Minn.)—History. 2. Saint
Paul (Minn.)—History.   I. Lanegran, David A.   II. Title.
F614.S4Y6   1996
977.6´581—dc20   96-14420
                                                            CIP

Second Printing 1997

Cover Photo: Chris LaFontaine

ISBN: 0-87839-105-3

Printed in the United States of America by Versa Press, Inc. of
East Peoria, Illinois.

Published by: North Star Press of St. Cloud, Inc.
                P.O. Box 451
                St. Cloud, Minnesota 56302

Dedication

To all the people who, over more than a century, have invested a part of their lives on Grand Avenue—

And to all those who work to preserve a sense of place and of the past in our largely homogenized urban environments.

Billie Young and David Lanegran

Contents

Preface by George Latimer ix

Introduction 1

Chapter 1   Carving a City from the Oak Savannah ... 5

Chapter 2   Trolley Technology and the Growth
             of Cities 11

Chapter 3   Having Fun on Grand Avenue 27

Chapter 4   Glamorous Gangsters on Grand 45

Chapter 5   What the Great War Did to Grand 53

Chapter 6   The I-94 Ditch and Its Urban Victims ... 59

Chapter 7   Urban Renewal: Government Efforts
             to Make Amends 67

Chapter 8   Historic Preservation to the Rescue 75

Chapter 9   Grand Avenue Organizes to
             Fight Blight 85

Chapter 10   A New Store Opens and Survives 95

Chapter 11   Victoria Crossing Comes to Grand 101

Chapter 12   First Bank Grand: The Uneasy
             Partner 113

Chapter 13   Mary Rice and Her Grand Old Ideas 119

Chapter 14   The Great Battle over Zoning 131

Chapter 15   Women Business Owners 145

Chapter 16   A Business Community Develops 157
Chapter 17   Franchises Find Grand Avenue 185
Chapter 18   Elements of Grand's Success 197
Appendix   Grand Avenue Business Association
                    Presidents 205
              Grand Avenue Business Association
                    Executive Directors 206

Preface

BECAUSE I SERVED AS MAYOR of the City of Saint Paul during many of the years of Grand Avenue renaissance, the authors of this book charged me with the task of giving the local public official view of that renaissance. I, of course, have ignored their charge (as often happens with old mayors) and prefer to speak from a personal and familial view.

For many of us, a trip down Grand Avenue is nothing if not personal. For the Latimer family, Grand was like a close friend, the link between home and the busy lives we led in the city. Grand is the street I raced down in 1967 to the old Children's Hospital where heroic, successful efforts saved the life of Tom, our youngest son. For our five children, Grand was the thoroughfare to their schools—St. Luke's Webster, Central, and, later, for two of them, Macalester College. Grand was where they and their friends found their first work for pay—hard work, washing dishes at the Uptowner, waiting tables at the Acropol, shoveling snow for various businesses, and clerking at Grand & Dale Pharmacy. Our eldest child, Faith, recalls waiting on tables at Aris and Sandy Apostolou's restaurant, the Acropol. She remembers Evie Omundson, an older waitress whom Aris and Sandy would drive home to her apartment above the drugstore each night after her shift. When Evie passed on after sixty years of sweet-tempered waitressing, all her friends gathered at Willwerscheid & Peters Funeral Home to celebrate her life of service on Grand Avenue. So the memories of Grand are personal and span whole lives, from the cradle to the grave.

Most of us never reflect on how Grand came to be such a place, where people young and old come to live, work, play and pray. This book tells the story of how Grand Avenue came to be the way it is, how it developed economically, socially and architecturally. One thing is clear—City Hall had little to do with the renaissance of Grand Avenue— at least not while I was there. Economics played a strong role. Surely the commercial strip lying between Summit Avenue, Ramsey Hill, and Crocus Hill could count on some disposable income coming its way, and much did. Architecture has shaped Grand's history as well: the delicate blending of human scale businesses with residences set Grand apart as a place of commerce *and* community, a feat no mall can hope to achieve. As with all good stories, it is the cast of characters that brings this street to life: entrepreneurs like James Wengler and Billie Young, colorful folks like Doc Chopp and Wally Peters, preservationists like Jim Linden and David Lanegran.

The collaboration between Billie Young and David Lanegran in telling this story was made in heaven. Only Billie, a risk-taker herself, could capture so well the story of lawyer Jim Stolpestad's almost casual entry into real estate by picking up Victoria Crossing for the proverbial "song" and patiently nurturing its status as commercial hub of the avenue. Only the discerning mind of geographer Lanegran could lead us through the issues of adaptive reuse, the transformation of Grand from car dealerships to the rich variety of marvelous and useful businesses that now line the avenue. Unifying their work is attention to detail, which is faithful to reality and a love of the stubborn, proud, resilient old street in this unique and liveable city.

There is no wonder why Grand works so well. The mix of work and play in close proximity to where we live is simply the way people have gathered themselves for nearly all of our recorded history. The fragmenting, isolating forces of malls, freeways, industrial parks, and bedroom communities, such powerful and standardized parts of contemporary American life, have existed for less than thirty years of long history—one-fifth of the life of Grand Avenue.

Yi-Fu Tuan, a renowned geographer and philosopher, has remarked that *place* is what is created when people add history and human experience to their environment. Is it any wonder that Grand Avenue feels more like home to us and why it remains an intensely personal place to so many of us?

George Latimer
former mayor of St. Paul

x

GRAND AVENUE

Horse-drawn delivery wag-
ons on Grand Avenue, 1914.
(Photo courtesy of Abbott
Paint Company.)

Introduction

THIS IS THE STORY OF A STREET, a street called Grand Avenue in St. Paul, Minnesota. A street is often considered of little consequence, the link between two points of greater interest, a set of parallel lines on a map, a kind of utility such as power and sewer lines extended into the suburbs to spur development.

Grand Avenue, a street in the inner city of St. Paul, Minnesota, runs east to west for about four miles, parallel to and a block south of its more illustrious neighbor, Summit Avenue.[1] Grand is lined with a mix of buildings, apartment houses, duplexes, private homes, small businesses, and mini-malls. It is a place of memories and of stories. Grand Avenue is where the boy Scott Fitzgerald went to dancing class, where the gangster and Public Enemy Number One John Dillinger attended the movies and where the generous credit policies of the Grand Avenue Market enabled some of the leading families of St. Paul to survive the Depression. Grand Avenue is where, during Prohibition, druggists on almost every corner dispensed 200-proof alcohol in gallon cans, thanks to the helpful prescriptions of cooperative doctors.

Because Grand is not a through street (it ends at Cretin Avenue on the west and begins at Seventh Street below the bluff on the east) traffic moves slowly. Cars park on both sides of the street, and there is almost, but not quite, enough room for two lanes of traffic to move in each direction. In the winter, when snowplows pile up the snow on the curbs, traffic is sometimes reduced to one lane in either direction. One of the authors was rear-ended one winter, her car sent plunging into a snow drift by a driver who had leaned over to put a can of pop on the floor and failed to observe that the car ahead had slowed to make a left turn into Knowlan's grocery store parking lot.

Like a Mayan pyramid, Grand Avenue is built on a foundation of its former self. Under the asphalt that surfaces the street is a layer of brick, the high-fired, rounded paving stones, as hard as granite, which the Victorians laid down when the avenue was first claimed from the prairie woodland. When the ground freezes and heaves in a particularly severe January, a brick will pop up from the ground—reminding those of us who know the story of the street that the past has not totally departed but is still there, sleeping through the decades under four inches of asphalt. David Lanegran, professor of geography at Macalester College, keeps one of these cast up bricks on his bookcase as a reminder.

A useful street is perceived as one that is straight, has no distractions or interruptions and allows traffic to move along it as rapidly as possible. Our words for streets imply movement. We call our big thoroughfares "arteries," and professional disciplines are devoted to the science of keeping those arteries unobstructed and free flowing.

The American view of a street is that it is a corridor for automobiles—that pedestrians and bicyclists are interlopers and intruders. A child's first lesson is to not stray into the street. Pedestrians are of such small concern that many streets do not even have sidewalks, and the solitary walker must face the traffic during his stroll, ready at any moment to leap into the ditch should a car contest his or her right to be on the road.

Other peoples in other places have seen the street as living room, theater, coffee shop, the place to display artistry in the laying of paving stones, the place to meet, the space in the city where one goes to see people and to be seen. The street for many centuries has been the place where the human encounter takes place.

In this context, the street is valued for qualities unrelated to the automobile. It is valued for the beauty and texture of its paving, its pleasant and unexpected vistas, its twists and turns, its sidewalk cafes, its flower boxes and newsstands, the elements that slow traffic rather than speed it up. Such a street develops on a human scale to meet human needs and not those of the machine.

The most significant streets in a Mexican village are those surrounding the town plaza. Here young people gather at dusk to promenade. The boys in their tight pants and slicked down hair saunter in one direction. The girls in flowered dresses and high heels, arms linked, slowly circle the plaza the opposite way. Parents push infants in strollers. Men exchange business cards and discuss deals. Venders sell tacos and peanuts, chewing gum and balloons, and the air is scented with the perfume of gardenias and burning charcoal. Older people stand in little groups to share news and opinions while keeping a watchful eye on the youth. For a few hours in the evening, the streets become community salons where transactions of all sorts take place—including the tentative opening moves of courtship rituals.

Left to their own devices—and if there is no threat of danger—people return automatically to the streets. That is where life and action are. How many parents have furnished a backyard with elaborate play equipment only to find their children spending an inordinate amount of time on the street? The biggest dispute on Grand Avenue (besides the parking) involves Grand Old Day—a half-day festival where tens of thousands of Twin Citians turn out to do nothing more than walk, eat (a few drink too much beer) and listen to music in the street. That activity has become suspect to those who fail to understand that the Grand Old Day revelers are returning to the activity for which city streets have always been intended—that of the serendipitous meeting and interacting with other people.

While Americans, enthralled by their romance with the automobile, have largely forgotten the many delights of being a pedestrian in an urban setting, European civilization has not. Walkways in cities have been covered with arcades and porticoes to provide shade and protection from the rain and thus make them more enjoyable for walking. In Greece, walking outdoors, under cover, was a feature of the philosophical school known as the "peripatetics" from "peripatos"—meaning literally "covered walkway" and referred to Aristotle's habit of conversing with his students while he walked with them through the streets.

The street as a site for dining has also been popular in Europe since ancient times. The genuine cafe is always part of the street, whether or not there is a sidewalk. To sit at a table in the open air and view the ever-changing street scene is theater that never tires. The French sociologist Chombart de Lauwe considers the sidewalk or street cafes indispensable to civilized city life. He sorts the cafes out according to their types of customers and locations, noting that there are cafes for sports enthusiasts, for poets, for lovers, cafes with a history, and cafes on busy or quiet streets.

Italians consider dining on the street a normal, everyday occurrence. In Mondelo, a suburb of Palermo, Sicily, tables spill out of the indoor portion of the cafes, across the sidewalk and into the street, leaving only a narrow corridor through which cars, moving slowly, can maneuver. Americans, who view the street as the exclusive province of automobiles, are amazed at the patience displayed by drivers and the nonchalance of diners and waiters as the cars painstakingly thread their way past the tables.

While a few streets have become part of the collective memory of western civilization (the Via Appia, for example, or Wall Street) others are known only in their community as being streets of uncommon interest. Why these streets achieve local fame is not immediately clear. In appearance they do not differ markedly from their neighbors. They are not wider, longer and do not, in most cases, have grander buildings bordering them. Yet these streets, at all hours of the day, have people on them, bikers and walkers and infants in baby carriages. There is an atmosphere that attracts strollers, an élan that defines them as something more than a transportation link connecting one part of a city to another. These streets have the personality and character of a neighborhood.

Did they become this way by accident? Are there clues to be found in the histories of successful streets that could guide present day urban planners? By taking a closer look at inner city streets that have succeeded can we discover the mysterious alchemy by which they have become a vital part of an urban village?

Such a street is Grand Avenue in St. Paul, Minnesota. One of the authors of this book is a professor at Macalester College, located on Grand Avenue, who for years has used the street as a laboratory for his urban geography students. The other author was in business on Grand Avenue for twenty-two years, from 1972, when the street was believed to be in a state of irreversible decline, to 1994 when Grand Avenue had become one of the most desirable commercial locations in the Twin Cities. How that transformation came about is the subject of this book.

Note

1. Summit Avenue is considered to be the best preserved Victorian monumental, residential boulevard in the United States.

1

Carving a City
from the Oak Savannah

GRAND AVENUE WAS PLATTED in 1871 as a part of the Summit Park subdivision of the City of St. Paul, Minnesota. Summit Park was a suburban addition to the city developed by two businessmen, William S. Wright from Cincinnati and John Wann from St. Louis. Everyone in St. Paul at that time was from someplace else. John Wann had been born in 1829 in Belfast, the son of the manager of the Bank of the North of Ireland. At the age of eighteen, he had gone to India to work for the East India Company. He left India for St. Louis in 1854 and came to St. Paul in 1865.

Wann is the man who gave Grand Avenue its name. As an Irish-Englishman, Wann may have had a lively relationship with his American wife because she insisted that he name several streets in his subdivision after important American Revolutionary events such as the battles of Lexington and Saratoga. Later, Wann was to build a large mansion on the corner of Victoria Street and Summit Avenue, a site at one time considered for the Cathedral. Wann ultimately sold the house to Bishop John Ireland. A cosmopolitan man, Wann took his two daughters to Europe in 1872 where one of them married into a titled family in Prussia.[1]

Little is known of Mr. Wright, one of many developers and land speculators attracted to the new town. Barely thirty years had passed since Father Lucian Galtier had built his log chapel in the frontier village and dedicated it to St.

Paul. At the time of the dedication, Galtier had suggested that the fledgling town take the same name. Fortunately, the citizens took his advice, averting the possibility that the community would be named Pig's Eye after a notorious 1830s saloon housed in a nearby riverside cave. The January 1, 1850, issue of the *Pioneer* attributed the following verse to James Goodhue.

> Pig's Eye, converted thou shalt be, like Saul;
> Arise, and be, henceforth, Saint Paul.[2]

The expansion of St. Paul followed the standard process of platting and subdivision common to all new towns in the west. Col. Henry Sibley and a group of partners had purchased the original town site from the federal government

Map showing Grand Avenue in relation to the Twin Cities metropolitan area. The street runs east and west, one block south of Summit Avenue. (David Lanegran map.)

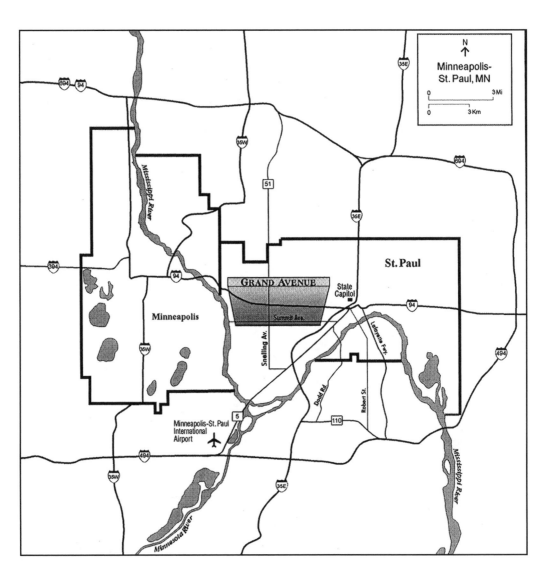

in the first public land auction after the treaties between the United States and the Lakota Indians were ratified. Once the town site was surveyed and the plat registered, other promoters surveyed and platted additions to the City of St. Paul.

In one sense, this development process was orderly. Land was surveyed, and plat maps were properly recorded; the city council voted approval of each new addition; streets were graded, and the market place determined how much, if anything, the city lots were worth. Yet the growth was not planned nor was it particularly contiguous. The settlement edge of St. Paul reached out spasmodically in fits and starts, as a reflection of the dreams and ambitions of individual promoters. In some places the subdivisions did not fit together well. Roads jogged and even changed names or orientation where the subdivisions abutted one another.

By the standards of the time, the developers did their best in considering the local topography when they laid out their subdivisions. But the landscape of St. Paul was hilly—chopped up by ravines—and did not easily lend itself to the imposition of a flat grid map. As a result, there was a great deal of cutting down of hills and filling in of depressions, creeks and stream beds.

Until the streets were platted and graded, roads followed the ravines so that travelers could take advantage of the gentle grade when climbing the bluffs. These old routes still exist and can be recognized because they cut across the grid of streets and lots to get to the river by the shortest possible route. Old routes such as Dodd Road-Stryker-Winifred Avenues, State Street, Oakland Avenue, St. Anthony-Rice Street, Jackson Street, and Mississippi Street lead people out of the valley and on to the upland all around the city core.

Few ravines, however, cut through the massive bluff west of the city, the site of Wann's and Wright's subdivision of Summit Park. The main path from the Falls of St. Anthony came down from the upland through a break in the cliffs between the present day cathedral and the Capitol. This was the main route of the Red River Fur Trade and the eventual alignment of the Territorial Road that ran west to Minneapolis.

Major fur trading had begun in the 1830s, and by 1845 fur-laden ox carts had established a permanent route from Pembina in northwestern Minnesota to St. Paul, where the furs could be loaded onto boats for shipment down the Mississippi. This was St. Paul's first encounter with transportation technology, and it made a significant impact on the growing city. Caravans of several hundred carts would arrive

A train of Red River ox carts on Main Street of St. Anthony, Minnesota, 1855. (Courtesy of Minnesota Historical Society.)

daily in the town. Each cart carried a load of 1000 pounds of buffalo hides and other furs. The drivers would unload the furs on the docks by the river and then load up their carts with supplies to take north.[3]

The carts themselves were extraordinary vehicles. Built entirely of wood, they were two-wheeled and were drawn by a single ox. No grease was used on the axles, and the screeching wheels could be heard for many miles over the prairies. Primitive as the carts were, they helped establish St. Paul as a major transportation and trading center in the northwest. Located at the head of navigation of the Mississippi River, St. Paul quickly became the region's first major commercial center. In 1849, it became the capitol of the Minnesota Territory and, with the admittance of the state to the Union in 1858, capitol of the state.

Wann and Wright were not the first real estate promoters to seek riches in developing the heights to the west of
the core of St. Paul. The high bluff overlooking the majestic
valley of the Mississippi had been occupied by suburbanites
since before the Civil War, but growth had been slow, and
the houses were few and isolated. There were still many
attractive sites close to the center of commerce. In 1853, J.
Wesley Bond and others predicted that the bluffs ringing the
river landing would be perfect places for high-class residential districts.

> "Nature never planned a spot better adapted to build up a showy
> and delightful display of architecture and gardening than that nat-
> ural terrace of hills," he wrote. A fellow enthusiast went on to say,
> "Indeed we seem to behold even now, through the dim vista of
> future years, the glittering mansions of St. Paul's merchant-princes
> rising up in every direction, on these hills now in a state of nature
> or rudely adorned by the humble chaumiere of the French and half-
> breeds, or the simple lodges of the noble Sioux."[4]

A photograph taken in 1859 shows six houses lining
the western bluff overlooking St. Paul. These houses were all
on Summit Avenue. The earliest house, built in 1855, was the
home of Edward Dufield Niell, the pastor of House of Hope
Church. Financial panics of the late 1850s and the Civil War
slowed St. Paul's growth.

Rebecca Marshall Cathcart, an early resident of the
area wrote:

> Summit Avenue was a lonely place at this time (1863). Between
> it and Selby Avenue stood a dense forest of native oaks, and the
> few houses were separated by large unoccupied grounds. Many and
> many a night after the Indian Massacre of 1862 have I lain awake
> listening for the Indian war whoop and think how easily they could
> come through the woods and kill us all.[5]

Wealthy households and realtors were lured by the
potential of developing the western edge of the city. This was
the upwind side of the town and was thought, because of
this, to be more healthy. While it certainly was less polluted,
the barrier of the bluff was a considerable obstacle. Only
twenty-four houses were built on the brow of the bluff along
Summit Avenue between 1855 and 1882. Rollin A. Lanpher
owned a house on Western and Dayton in the early 1870s.
He wrote:

> It was difficult to get into the hill district from down town; there
> was then no Oakland Avenue and no Ramsey Street. We reached
> our homes either by going up Third Street hill, or by going first to
> Rice Street, and then up Summit Avenue. In winter it was espe-
> cially hard.[6]

Further west, the streets drawn on the plat maps had not been built. Giles W. Merrill built a home in the 600 block on Laurel in 1871. He reported that there were only two houses further west than his.

> There were no roads or streets leading to my home then. We simply lived in the country. In the early eighties streets began to be laid out and people gradually settled about us.[7]

Notes

1. *St. Paul Dispatch*, August 24, 1905. See also *St. Paul Pioneer Press*, August 27, 1905. Elberta Matters, *Grand Avenue Promenade* (Emporium Press, St. Paul, Minnesota, 1977).

2. J. Fletcher Williams, *History of the City of St. Paul to 1875* (Minnesota Historical Society Press, St. Paul, Minnesota, 1983), p. 113.

3. Ted Lentz, *Selby Avenue—Status of the Street* (St. Paul, Minnesota, Old Town Restorations, Inc. 1978), p. 4.

4. Robert Ernest Sandeen, *St. Paul's Historic Summit Avenue* (Living Historical Museum, Macalester College, St. Paul, Minnesota, 1978), p. 1.

5. Sandeen, p. 3.

6. Sandeen, p. 6.

7. Sandeen, p. 6.

2

Trolley Technology and the Growth of Cities

BY 1865 ST. PAUL HAD a population of 12,976 and was the largest city in Minnesota. Minneapolis at the time was one third the size of St. Paul with a population of 4,607.[1] The Civil War had ended, and the city was poised for major expansion. The flow of immigrants into the upper Mississippi Valley was increasing as was the population of St. Paul. The western city limit of St. Paul was Dale Street, and the residents of Summit Avenue paid an assessment to have their street graded to Dale. Very few people lived beyond Dale Street. That would change in 1871 when the Summit Park addition was platted and the city limit was expanded one mile west to Lexington.

In that same year, the city council hired the great landscape architect Horace W.S. Cleveland to come to St. Paul from Chicago to make recommendations for city improvement. When he arrived and looked about him, Cleveland was upset that more of the city's natural beauty had not been maintained. He disapproved of the row of mansions blocking the view over the valley from Summit Avenue and believed that the bluff should have been preserved as a public park so that everyone would have an opportunity to enjoy the magnificent views of the Mississippi River and the hills beyond.

"If the avenue had only been carried near the edge of the bluff and no building allowed except on the opposite side, what a strikingly beautiful feature this might have been. As

11

it is," a frustrated Cleveland complained, "one is simply tantalized by an occasional glimpse of the portion of it between the trees on the private grounds which intervene."[2]

Despite the presence of the bluff and the view over the river valley, the developers had followed a grid design, turned Summit sharply away from the river bluff where the University Club now stands and ran the avenue down the middle of the Summit Park development. While he could not undo the past, Cleveland had a bold vision of the future and called for construction of a wide boulevard from the city limits to the Mississippi gorge and the western border of Ramsey

Detail of the 1892 *Donnelly Atlas*, showing farms extending from Snelling to the river. (Laura Church and Dave Lanegran photo.)

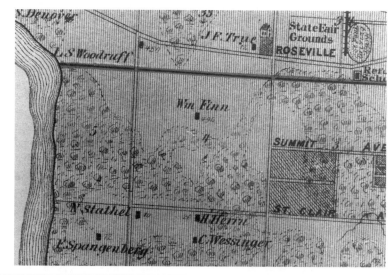

The intersection of Lexington and Summit Avenues, looking west. Taken about 1900. (Courtesy of the Minnesota Historical Society.)

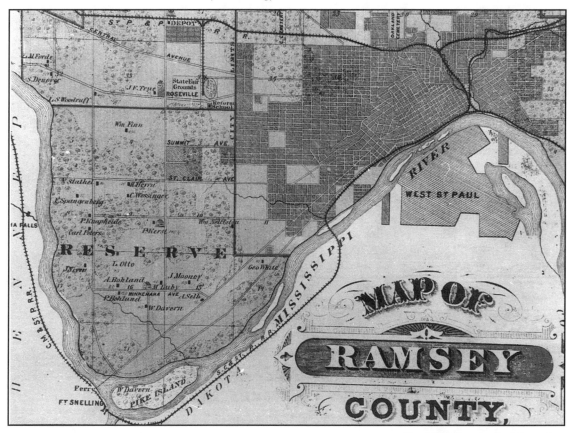

The 1892 *Donnelly Atlas of St. Paul*, showing the city limit on the west at Lexington Avenue. Summit extended on to Snelling, but Grand ended at the Macalester College campus. (Laura Church and Dave Lanegran photo.)

County. His dream had to wait because Wann and Wright and the other developers of additions east of Lexington, while they may have agreed with Cleveland in theory, refused to use their land to widen Summit Avenue within the boundaries of their subdivisions.

The *Andreas Historical Atlas of Minnesota*, published in 1874, provides an image of the Grand Avenue corridor on the verge of major growth. The streets were platted all the way to the city limits at Lexington and given names that evoked images of prestige and genteel life styles. The developers were anticipating continued growth of the city into Reserve Township, which lay west of the city. Some platting beyond the city limits had occurred. Marson and Simonton's addition of 1872 consisted of an area west of Lexington to the shoreline ravine and south from Summit to St. Clair.[3]

By 1874, only two blocks along Grand—running west from Lexington to Griggs—had been developed. Beyond them, a speculator named Stinson owned a large tract of land that had no settlements on it. Next to it was Cavender's development, bounded by Hamline Avenue, Summit

Avenue, Snelling, and St. Clair. This area was bisected by Goodrich, and the resulting lots were very large, roughly two and one-half to three times the size of other lots inside the city. A large woods extended west from Lexington to the river gorge consisting of a relatively open oak forest mixed with areas of long-grass prairie. Beyond the zone of speculation lay the farm of William Finn (which extended from Snelling toward the river gorge) about half of which appeared to be cultivated.[4]

In addition to being a speculator in real estate, John Wann was the vice-president of the St. Paul Street Railway Company. His partner, Wright, was a fellow board member. It had not escaped their attention that it would be much easier to sell property in their subdivision of Summit Park up on the bluffs if there were a means of transportation that could carry residents downtown for work and then return them to their homes on the hill. Horse-drawn trolleys might be an answer, they reasoned, allowing people of modest means a way to own their own homes in the new developments and still be able to get downtown to work.

The St. Paul Street Railway Company was organized by a group of St. Paul businessmen in 1872. Bonds were sold to construct track and buy horses and cars. Though the horse cars turned out to be popular with riders, they were not a comfortable means of transportation. Not many of the streets had been paved nor, for the most part, had they been graded. The tracks were laid on the streets, rough and rutted as they were. Wooden stringers of five-inch by five-inch lumber were spiked to cross ties. Iron plates weighing twenty-three

A horse car. The picture was taken somewhere in St. Paul, ca. 1860s. (Photo courtesy of the Minnesota Historical Society.)

pounds for every yard were nailed to the stringers, forming rails. One mile of completed track cost $6,000.[5]

The cars that rode on these rails measured ten feet long, weighed approximately 1000 pounds and were limited by the St. Paul city council to a top speed of six miles per hour. In winter, the floors of the cars were insulated with a foot of hay to help keep the passengers' feet warm, and a small iron stove provided additional heat. A smelly oil lamp hung in each car, which carried fourteen passengers on benches that ran along the sides. The fare was five cents or six rides for a quarter. On boarding, passengers would drop their nickels into a fare box in the front. If one forgot, the driver would stamp on a gong to remind him. Derailments were frequent. When a car went off the tracks, the passengers were expected to get out and help the driver get it back on the rails.

For wages of thirty-five dollars per month, the driver sat outside on an open, exposed platform and drove the car for fifteen hours each day with one twenty-minute break for dinner. The driver was also expected to keep his car washed down, inside and out. Each car was pulled by one horse, but it took six horses to keep the cars running for a fifteen-hour day. Mules were also used, but mules would balk—sometimes for up to an hour at a time. Riders were patient, offering advice to the driver on how to get the mule started up again.

Though the horse-drawn trolleys were well-accepted by their riders, the business lost money, and in 1877 the properties were foreclosed by a group of thirteen New York bondholders. The assets included three and three-quarters miles of track, fifteen cars, thirty-four horses, six mules, twenty-four horse collars, fourteen bridles, horse blankets, buffalo robes, nine coal stoves for the cars, and two mouth rasps for the horses' teeth.[6]

The new owners hoped to solve the financial problems of the horse cars by raising fares, increasing the cost of a ride from five to six cents. This plan failed when an over-zealous driver threw a woman off one of the cars when she did not have the extra penny. The woman sued, was awarded $200 damages, and the owners promptly put the fares back to a nickel.

In 1883, discouraged over the continued losses, the stockholders in the St. Paul Railroad Company sold all of their stock to a young man from Minneapolis who clearly understood the relationship between street rail lines and urban development. The young man was Thomas Lowry, a lawyer from Logan County, Illinois, who, just two years before, had become the sole owner of the Minneapolis Street Railway Company.

Lowry was twenty-four when he came to Minneapolis in 1867. He was a tall, lean man with an angular frame and bore a resemblance to Abraham Lincoln, whom he greatly admired. Lincoln had done legal work for Lowry's father in Illinois, and, as a fifteen-year-old, Lowry had attended one of the Lincoln-Douglas debates. Lowry had not been in Minneapolis long before he realized that his future lay in real estate speculation, not in law, and he began buying up city lots and tracts of land throughout Minneapolis and St. Paul. He was greatly helped in this activity by his marriage to Beatrice, the sixteen-year-old daughter of Dr. Calvin Gibson Goodrich, a wealthy resident of Minneapolis.[7]

When the financial panic of 1873 hit, commercial activity in the two cities came to a temporary halt. Though real estate prices held fairly steady compared to other communities, there was little activity. Few people were buying or selling. Casting about for a way to create interest in the large tracts of property he and his father-in-law owned, Lowry looked to street railway transportation as a way of developing outlying areas. As had taken place in St. Paul, Minneapolis investors, including Lowry, raised the capital to build a Minneapolis horse drawn trolley system. And, as had happened in St. Paul, the business lost money. Lowry, alone of the investors, had faith in the system. Though the trolley company lost money, the system grew. By 1890, St. Paul had 159 horse cars and 900 horses covering 53.3 miles of track. Minneapolis had 218 horse cars and 1,018 horses operating over 66.7 miles of track.[8]

By 1886, Lowry was deeply in debt with a transportation business that, despite its popular success, continued to lose money. To raise capital, he sold most of his stock in the two street railway companies to a Boston syndicate, selling the Minneapolis stock for forty-five dollars a share and that of St. Paul for twenty-five dollars. Lowry stayed on as manager, struggling to find a way to make the business profitable.

Without some new technology, it appeared to be an impossible task. The purchase and maintenance of a horse cost $200 per year. The new, larger cars required a total of twelve horses to move one car through a fifteen-hour day, making the total power cost for one car per year $2,400. Management was also acutely aware that it could not raise the fares above the five cent per ride rate. Five cents was a lot of money for men earning just one dollar a day.

The financial problems of street railway companies were not unique to Minneapolis and St. Paul. Inventors all over the country were scrambling for solutions to the problem of how to provide urban transportation at a cost lower than could be provided by horses. One system that initially showed promise was a steam-powered cable car. A moving cable could be installed in the street, powered by a nearby steam generator. A grip on the bottom of the car grasped the cable enabling it to be pulled along the street. While the installation cost was high, the operating cost was half that of horses. Lowry decided to try cable.

In 1887, the first cable line in Minnesota was built by Lowry in St. Paul. It ran from Broadway west on Fourth and Third Streets, up the bluff, (a sixteen percent grade), and out Selby Avenue to St. Albans. (A second cable line of about the same length was completed in June 1889 and ran from Wabasha Street out Seventh Street to Duluth Avenue.) A steam powerhouse was built on the site of the horsecar barns at Dale and Selby, and the line opened for business on January 16, 1888.[9]

Hundreds of people lined up to ride the new steam cable car, which ran at the great speed of ten miles per hour. At the Selby Avenue section of the ride, where the car climbed the bluff, passengers were so impressed by the capability of the cars that they rode up the hill on the cable car, got off, walked down the hill, and got back on the car for the ride up the hill again.

Just a few days after the successful opening of the line, on January 27, a grip failed to hold a car coming down the grade and the car ran off the racks, killing one passenger and seriously injuring several more. Though the cable line was later extended to Selby and Fairview in 1890, only eleven cars ever plied the route.[10]

The cable car with trailer that ran up Selby Hill in St. Paul, 1894. (Courtesy of the Minnesota Historical Society.)

During the decade of the 1880s, St. Paul turned into a boom town. As many as 500 people a day were arriving at the St. Paul docks. The population jumped from 41,473 in 1880 to 111,473 in 1885 and to 133,156 in 1890, the biggest growth spurt in its history. Houses were being built by the thousands. Macalester College and St. Thomas Aquinas Seminary were founded at the western edge of town and, to incorporate its growing suburbs, the city extended its boundaries from Lexington Avenue west to the Mississippi River. The city was growing and the direction that growth took was determined in large part by the trolley lines.

Lowry, Wright, and Wann were not the only people who grasped the significance of the relationship between transportation and land development. Two men who shared this insight were real estate developer Thomas Cochran and Archbishop John Ireland. Cochran, a founder of Macalester College, along with other college trustees, owned large tracts of land in the area. He had been born in New York in 1843, graduated in law, and came to St. Paul in 1868 for his health. Although he initially joined an insurance firm, he, like Lowry, found speculation in real estate more to his liking. Cochran was a Macalester trustee and worked for years fund raising for the college during its early financial struggles.

John Ireland was born in Ireland in 1838 and came to St. Paul when he was eleven years old. He studied in France between 1853 and 1861 but returned to St. Paul and was chaplain of the Fifth Minnesota Regiment during the Civil War. Later he became rector of St. Paul Cathedral and, in 1884, became Bishop. When St. Paul became an archdiocese in 1888, Ireland became the archbishop.

Ireland, like Cochran, was investing in land and founded St. Paul Seminary, which, along with Macalester College, was located west of the city in a wooded area surrounded by farms and fields. Both Cochran and Ireland wanted to sell their land and see the area developed. A commentator in *Northwest* magazine described the area in April, 1890:

> Reserve township with its groves of oaks and elms, its hills commanding extensive views over both cities which form the dual metropolis of the northwest, its winding roads, its bold wooded cliffs along the river, deeply creased with picturesque ravines where little streams leap over the brown rocks and hide in the thickets of ferns and flowering shrubs is, indeed, one vast natural parcel. It lies at the doors of both St. Paul and Minneapolis, but owing to the want of transportation by which it could be reached, it has until recently been as rural and apparently as remote as if it had been one hundred miles away.[11]

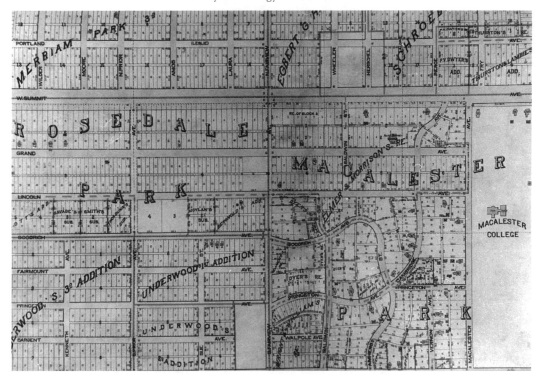

The 1892 *Donnelly Atlas of St. Paul,* showing Grand Avenue before it was cut through the Macalester campus. (Laura Church and Dave Lanegran photo.)

In the spring of 1889, Cochran and Ireland put together a group of investors to "build, equip and operate two electric lines" one of which was ". . . Grand to Cleveland as an extension of the existing horsecar line to Victoria and Grand." The connecting route to the downtown, from Victoria east, was to be electrified by Lowry's St. Paul Street Railway Company, which would be the contractor for the entire route. Cochran and Ireland named their company The Reserve Electric Motor Project and opened an office in St. Paul to handle the funds. Macalester College, at Cochran's urging, made a gift of $6,500 to the project and gave a right-of-way, 660 by eighty feet, through its property. Grand Avenue would now continue west to the seminary without interruption.[12]

The company plan called for property owners along the route to be assessed as the rails were laid down. There was no guarantee that the project would be feasible. Electricity had just begun to be used to power trolley cars. Lowry, when first approached by Cochran and Ireland, had been so skeptical of the practicality of electricity for the railway that he agreed to participate in the project only if his company would be indemnified if there were any loss.

The commercial success of the project depended on Lowry's ability to raise 2.5 million dollars of financing. He went to New York to sell bonds for the companies and found that, while the Minneapolis bonds found buyers, no one would buy the bonds for the St. Paul Street Railway Company, which had a lower ridership. Unless Lowry could sell bonds for both companies, he would not be able to raise enough money to build the system. At the last minute a solution was found by a New York banker named J. Kennedy Todd, who suggested the idea of putting all the bonds into one unified company. In this way the Minneapolis bonds would help support the St. Paul issue.

Out of that idea was born the Twin City Rapid Transit Company. The first electric trolley line in St. Paul opened for business on February 22, 1890. The car was an open one, pulling a trailer and crowded with bowler-hatted civic leaders. From the picture taken at the time, it is not possible to discern a single woman in the group. Among the men were the governor, John Merriam, Archbishop John Ireland, and Thomas Lowry, president of the combined St. Paul and Minneapolis street railway companies.[13]

Crowds lined the route of the cars but not without some trepidation. People were fearful of the sparks shooting out from under the wheels, concerned that horses would be electrocuted if they stepped on the tracks and worried that

The opening of the Grand Avenue streetcar line, February 22, 1890. (Courtesy of the Minnesota Historical Society.)

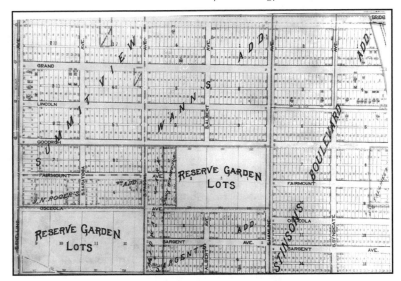

Map taken from the 1892 *Donnelly Atlas* of St. Paul, showing the locations of the Reserve Garden lots between Hamline and Snelling Avenues as well as the developers' divisions. (Laura Church and Dave Lanegran photo.)

the electrified cars would attract lightning during a thunderstorm. When the first car reached Macalester College, flag-waving students and faculty lined the route to greet it. A cannon was fired from Fort Snelling, and, when the car reached the end of the line at Cretin, the seminary band was on hand to play.

Despite the initial fears, the cars were immediately popular. Within a year from the introduction of the electric trolleys, the horse-drawn cars pulled into the barn for the last time. And, as predicted, development followed the iron rails. The oak forest was removed, tree by tree, as houses were built and streets platted. Stinson developed his property as the Stinson Boulevard Addition and created smaller lots for middle-class households. Further west, Wann actively developed several parcels, including the Summit View Addition. The huge lots Cavendar had platted persisted as Reserve Garden lots. Only six of the 300- by 500-foot lots remained in 1892. The others had been divided into smaller lots as dreams for an exclusive neighborhood faded.

In 1892, riders on the streetcar would have passed sixty-seven houses (there were twenty more on Grand east of Dale), two schools (Irving Elementary, at Grotto, and Alexander Ramsey, at Cambridge), a commercial block and Macalester College on their ride to Hill Seminary (St. Thomas University) at the end of the line. The trolley ride down Grand Avenue was looked on by the riders as an excursion into the country. The streetcar enabled the middle class to travel to the outskirts of the city and take advantage of recreational opportunities. Riders would bring picnic lunches and baseballs and ride out to St. Thomas Seminary for an afternoon baseball game. *Northwest* magazine reported on the Sunday ride to the country.

> On holidays and Sundays and the long summer evenings, the cars are crowded with lovers of nature, eager to escape for a little while from the brick walls and the paved streets, to breathe the pure air of the country and to wander under green boughs. It is a very orderly crowd for there are no amusements—no games and no saloons—at the end of the route to attract the rough elements of the city's population.
>
> Once up the hill the train turns on to Grand Avenue, here a pleasant shady street with more vacant lots than dwellings and a general air of village quiet. The dwellings are rarer and newer as you advance. A little stretch of open prairie is crossed, then a bridge over the shortline tracks which run to Minneapolis, and just beyond, the broad avenue cuts through a noble grove of oaks. Macalester is soon reached with its group of handsome red college buildings, its rows of pretty villas where live the professors and other people who are fond of living in the shadow of institutional learning and who appreciate the beauty of the landscape.[14]

On weekdays, residents of Grand Avenue rode the trolley to and from work in the downtown and often home for lunch as well. The cars ran every five minutes on Grand between the hours of 7:00 to 8:30 A.M., from 12:00 noon to 2:00 P.M. and from 5:00 P.M. to 8:00 P.M. at night.

The pattern of development along Grand was remarkably uneven. While some buildings stood at intersections, most corners were not built up. There was a marked absence of commercial buildings, apartment houses, or duplexes. This was in sharp contrast with Selby Avenue, six blocks north, which had many very large structures, including a curling club and power house for the streetcars. In those early years, no one expected Grand Avenue to become a bustling commercial artery.

The new electric line at Macalester College and Summit Avenue. (From *Northwest* magazine, July 1890, courtesy of the Minnesota Historical Society.)

Though the trolley was the engine that drove St. Paul development westward, on Grand Avenue itself, the trolley with its clanging bells and noisy iron wheels on the rails kept real estate prices lower than on neighboring streets. Houses were both very large and modest. Few were built of brick, and none were stone. There were fewer carriage barns in the backyards of the houses on Grand than on Summit Avenue, but many of the houses were substantial.

The Frank A. Eldredge family, owners of the Towle Maple Syrup Company, lived in an eighteen-room house at 777 Grand Avenue. The house featured a lighted skating rink and tennis court for the eleven Eldredge children, ten boys and a girl. The skating rink became a gathering place for neighborhood children who helped flood the rink by carrying water in Towle maple syrup cans. The Eldredge children and their friends also delighted in putting oil on the trolley tracks so they could watch the cars slide when they hit the slippery rails.[15]

The first trolley cars had been purchased in the East, but they were continually breaking down. After a few years of making repairs, the company began manufacturing its own cars. This proved so successful that, in 1907, the production was expanded and moved from Minneapolis to St. Paul onto a sixty-acre tract of land bordered by Snelling, University, Pascal, and St. Anthony.[16]

The standard car was forty-two feet long and seated fifty people. It was painted bright yellow with a brown roof. The seats were yellow wicker, and the woodwork was red mahogany. Iron gates closed off the back platform. The cars were clean and meticulously maintained. The windows, when they were lowered, dropped into a slot in the wall. Riders recall that the windows were easy to put down, but hard to get back up again when it began to rain. The floors of the cars were wood, and signs admonished passengers not to spit on them.

The motormen operated the cars with a removable handle inserted in a control box on the back platform. As they drove, they would call out the names of the streets. At the end of the line, the motorman switched the track by sticking a long rod with a flat end through a hole in the floor of the car to pry the tracks apart and accomplish the switch. The car had to be positioned just right to do this, and, in winter, when the switches were frozen, it could be a difficult task. Once the switch was thrown, an elaborate ceremony changed the long trolley arms from front to back. Power for the trolley was supplied from a pole set in the middle of the tracks. A cross arm was mounted on the pole from which the power lines were strung.[17]

By 1894, the trolley cars were doing double duty as traveling post offices. Iron mail boxes, similar to those on the street, were mounted on the right sides of the trolley cars so that patrons wanting to deposit mail could do so without boarding the cars. Postal employees emptied the boxes at each end of the line. Though the mail service was later discontinued, newspapers, packages, and pouch mail continued to be carried in the front vestibule of trolley cars until 1951.

Nineteen twenty-two was the peak year for the trolley cars. That year 226 million passengers rode the cars. Until the mid 1930s, each car was run by two crewmen, a motorman and a conductor. During the Depression and when the trolleys began to face competition from buses, the motorman was taken off, and the conductor had to do it all—sell tokens, make change, punch transfers, run the car, ring the bell and blast on the air horn whenever another vehicle, dog, child, or bicycle got in the way of the trolley.

Notes

1. Lentz, p. 5.

2. James Taylor Dunn, *Grand Gazette*, December 1973.

3. Illustrated Historical Atlas of State of Minnesota, *Andreas Historical Atlas* (A.T. Andreas, Chicago, 1874), p. 39.

4. Cavender and Stinson development.

5. Goodrich Lowry, *Street Car Man—Tom Lowry and the Twin City Rapid Transit* (Lerner Publications, Minneapolis, Minnesota,1978), p. 57.

6. Lowry, p. 57.

7. Lowry, p. 6. Thomas Lowry may have been married once before his marriage to the sixteen-year-old Beatrice. On July 11, 1870, a deed conveying the first lot Lowry had ever owned to Dr. Calvin Gibson Goodrich was signed by Tom and Harriet Lowry, his wife. On July 20, 1870, Lowry sold a substantial house for $5,000, the same amount he had paid for it just three months before. Within five months of the house sale, he was married to the wealthy Goodrich's daughter. Fifty years later, two friends of Lowry's, Clinton Morrison and Dr. H.H. Kimball, each claimed to have been the best man for Lowry at his wedding. Could there have been two marriages? If there were, there is no record in Hennepin County of a marriage of Tom Lowry to Harriet.

8. Lowry, p. 87.

9. Lowry, p. 104.

10. Lentz, p. 9.

11. *Northwest* magazine, 1890.

12. Lowry, p. 104.

13. Lowry, p. 115.

14. *Northwest* magazine, 1890, n.p.

15. Emily S. Lemon, "Historical Study of Grand Avenue, 1880 to Present," term paper, Macalester College, St. Paul, Minnesota, 1958, p. 44.

16. *Electric Railways of Minneapolis and St. Paul*, "Twin City Lines" (Interurbans, Los Angeles, California, 1953), p. 5.

17. Lowry, p. 156.

The Oxford Club on Grand Avenue between Lexington and Oxford. (Photos by J.W.G. Dunn, January 1917. Courtesy of the Minnesota Historical Society.)

3

Having Fun on Grand Avenue

BY THE EARLY 1900S GRAND AVENUE, from the top of the bluff on the east to well past Lexington on the west, had been filled in with houses. The side streets south to St. Clair were also built up, and the area was full of families with young children. Many of these children gravitated to an unusual topographical feature on Grand Avenue—a hollow caused by the melting of the prehistoric ice sheet. The depression was about thirty to forty feet deep and ran along the south side of Grand Avenue between Oxford and Lexington for about the width of an alley. This deep ravine became a favorite sledding hill for neighborhood residents in winter. Run-off water formed a small pond that, when frozen, was used for skating. In summer, enough water collected at the bottom for children to float rafts. Just two buildings bracketed the hollow, the Otto G. Peters house at 1042 Grand and Anna H. Sweeney's confectionery shop at the corner of Grand and Lexington.

On November 6, 1916, the ravine was incorporated as the Oxford Club "to promote social intercourse among its members as to the benefits which may be derived from physical exercise of all kinds." The favored sports were skating, tobogganing, and hockey. Early enthusiasts were Daniel P. Whyte at 1058 Lincoln, Carl D. Swendson at 1008 and Ned Bailie. Among the signers of the purchase agreement for the ravine were J. Norman Storr, president of Kuhles and Stock, cigar manufacturers; John W.G. Dunn, of Cushing, Dunn

27

and Driscoll, Realtors, at 1033 Lincoln; and Henry H. Flor, an attorney. During the early years, the land on which the hollow was located was rented from Rufus Jefferson, but, in 1923, the club bought the property.

The club had a fifteen-member board of directors, and, at its height, claimed 500 family members. Annual dues were five dollars per family, a sum later raised to eight dollars. Capital improvements were made to the site, including a bandstand and the warming house. John W.G. Dunn was secretary and gatekeeper at the long flight of wooden stairs that led from Grand Avenue down to the warming house and ice rink. He was also the disciplinarian, once kicking a youth named Neal Tilton off the rink for putting sneezing powder on the pot bellied stove of the warming house. The Oxford Club was popular and in use all day and every night. On weekend nights band music accompanied the skating, and the area was lit with hundreds of Japanese lanterns.[1]

A convenient source of refreshments was Sweeney's Confectionery Store, one of two run by the Sweeney sisters: Ann, who ran the store near the rink, and Mary B., who ran a similar store at 858 Grand. The two sisters were a familiar sight on the street as they carried merchandise back and forth between the stores. Ann kept her homemade ice cream in three-foot-tall tins, and dumped the ice water from her ice cream making out her back door into the western end of the Oxford Club ravine, where it would freeze in winter. The younger children used the incline for a sliding hill, scooting down thirty feet or more on sheets of cardboard.[2]

For more than a decade, the Oxford Club drew skaters and sledders to Grand Avenue. Then memberships began to drop, and 1927-1928 became the final season for the skating rink. In November 1928, a "sheriff's mortgage foreclosure sale" of the property was held, and the Oxford Club went out of existence. The warming shack and the bandstand burned down, and the hollow—scooped out ages before by a melting glacier—was doomed. Dump trucks brought in dirt and filled up the ravine. The first building to be built on the site created by the land fill was Pearl P. Gilbert's (later Pont's) Tea Room. Though the tea room is now gone, the building still stands and houses a branch office of Edina Realty.

Though Grand had originally been a residential street of single family houses in a variety of sizes, that was about to change. The presence of the streetcar running down the middle of the street and the proximity to the downtown made Grand Avenue a good location for apartment houses. The

Apartment buildings, both at Grand and Dale Streets. The one on the left shows the typical utilitarian brick structure, and the one on the right has spindle porches. (David Lanegran photos.)

first permit to build an apartment building on Grand Avenue was issued in 1889 for a "double dwelling" at 639-641 Grand Avenue. Several permits for flats (three-story apartment houses) at Dale and Grand were given between 1903 and 1905. The next surge in apartment building came after World War I and continued into the 1920s. Almost all of the apartments on Grand were completed before the 1930s. The city directory for that year lists approximately 100 apartments on Grand Avenue.

The apartment buildings on Grand Avenue are utilitarian brick rectangles, three stories high that front solidly on the street. Some have spindle porches, but most present a solid wall of brick, broken only by the front door to the street. The apartments brought more residents to Grand, and the growing population needed goods and services. Moreover, they needed these shops and service people close to their homes as many did not have a private means of transportation and rode the trolley cars to move about the city. The 1930 city directory lists 133 businesses on Grand between number 617 (a Piggly-Wiggly grocery) near Dale Street and number 1702, (Hugh Koenig's bakery) just past Macalester College. There were tinners and tailors, beauty shops and barbers, dressmakers, tailors, and furriers.

One of the first commercial buildings to go up on the street was that of the F.W. Ramaley Company, constructed in 1901 at 664-668 Grand Ave. The company had begun business at the Angus Hotel at Selby and Western Avenues before moving to Grand. The first floor of the building housed a large catering service, bakery, and delicatessen. The second floor was known as Ramaley Hall where parties, balls, and dance classes were held. (Mary Wilson has a picture of a

Professor Baker's dance class, Ramaley Hall, April 1910. First row: McNeil Seymour, Leonard Shepley, Archibald Jackson, Hamilton Hersey, Betty Mudge, Eleanor Mitchell, Cecil Read, Henry Adams, Truman Gardner; second row: Dorothy Green, Kitty Schultz, Margaret Horn (Russell), Egbert Driscoll, Elizabeth Field (Stryker), Marie Hersey, Alida Bigelow (Butler), Helen James, Margaret Armstrong, Julia Dorr, Joanne Orton, Professor Baker; third row: Donald Driscoll, Jim Porterfield, Arhur Foley, Larry Boardman, Georgia Ingersoll (Lewis), Susanne Rice, Caroline Clark, Donald Bigelow, Robert Clark, Dorothy Anderson, Jean Ingersoll, Gus Schurmeier; fourth row: Ted Townsend, Jack Mitchell, Mildred Bishop, Priscilla Adams, Wharton Smith, Theodore Ames, Elizabeth Devin, Catherine Ordway, Philip Stringer, Lowell May, and F. Scott Fitzgerald. (Photo courtesy of the Minnesota Historical Society.)

children's ballroom dancing class taken in 1910 at Ramaley Hall. Among the students is her father, Philip Stringer, and the writer, F. Scott Fitzgerald.) Ramaley's had a full-time staff of thirty and a part-time staff of hundreds of waiters and bartenders as well as a carriage man in a frock coat and top hat who directed the carriage traffic. As many as fifty carriages would be parked and waiting outside Ramaley Hall when large parties were being held.[3]

For the first three decades of the century, Ramaley's was famous for its food and is still remembered for its perfect chocolate éclairs and homemade mayonnaise. (The mayonnaise was kept fresh in a huge vat from which it was scooped out into cartons for customers.)

Mary E. Hoffman remembered that Ramaley's

sold home-baked beans, potato salad, and other deli items. The French pastries were seven-layer marvels of thin, thin slices of sponge cake layered with creamy fillings. The pastries were covered with finely ground nuts and topped with frosting flowerettes, and trying to eat one out-of-hand was like dealing with a handful of mashed potatoes. The pastries' freshness and delicacy demanded the refinement of a plate and fork. But we tried, we tried, wobbling along with one hand on the bike handlebars and the other being licked clean, germs and all.[4]

Entire holiday meals were prepared by the chefs for take-out. On Christmas morning, the chauffeur-driven Packards and Pierce Arrows, successors to the carriages, were double-parked on Grand while their uniformed drivers

Ramaley Hall with the Crocus Hill Food market, ca. 1956. (Photo courtesy of the Minnesota Historical Society.)

picked up immense roast turkeys, mashed potatoes, Parker House rolls, chestnut dressing, and plum pudding for the holiday feasts.

The early 1920s was the brief period of the electric car on Grand Avenue. The electric car, made in 1914 by the Rauch and Lang Company, was considered a "lady's car," and no man would ever willingly be seen driving one. The interiors of the cars were upholstered in a pearl-gray plush. Seats were arranged so the passengers faced each other as in a living room, and a crystal bud vase with a single fresh flower stood in a bracket by the door. The cars were high, requiring a step up to get into them, and had big windows all around. The driver, always a dignified lady in hat and gloves, sat at one side and steered with a tiller bar. The maximum speed was eight miles an hour, and the cars ran for about four hours on a single charge.

For recharging, the cars were taken for the night to the Detroit Electric Car Company garage at Grand and Milton. In the morning, a mechanic in a duster would deliver the cars to their owners who, if they were not in too great a rush, would give the mechanic a ride back to the garage. There were probably no more than a half-dozen electric cars

Byers-Patro Motor Company (left) at Grand and Victoria. This building is now Victoria Crossing South. The photo was taken about 1927 or 1928. Berry Chevrolet Company (right) at 871-873 Grand Avenue, about 1926. (Photos courtesy the Minnesota Historical Society.)

on Grand Avenue, but they contributed greatly to the local scene, gliding silently down the street like gracious movable tea parties.

Grand Avenue in the 1920s and 1930s was St. Paul's automobile row, where cars whose names have been forgotten could be purchased. Bingham and Norton sold Reos, "Floating Power" cars, and later Plymouths at 851-857 Grand where Victoria Crossing East is now located. Across the street, in the building where Cafe Latte and Ciatti's are presently housed, was a major Studebaker dealership where one could also buy an Erskine. At 758 Grand, where Walgreen's drugstore is, was the Twin City Motor Car Company on whose premises auto enthusiasts could examine a Hudson, an Essex, an Overland or a Willy's Knight—"the car that improves with age."

One Grand Avenue car dealer became a St. Paul hero. He was Ned Warren who had the Warren-Given Buick agency at 917 Grand. He later took over the Malmon Pontiac agency at 734 Grand in the building that presently houses the White Lily Restaurant. The teamster's union, which was believed to be associated with organized crime at the time, threatened Warren, and he responded by setting up a .30 caliber machine gun on the roof of his business, right over the front door on Grand Avenue. The community was so impressed with his show of courage and defiance that he was named Commissioner of Public Safety, the civilian official who served as the head of the St. Paul police department in reform-mayor Mark Gehan's administration.[5]

Selby Avenue also had some car dealerships, but the owners guessed wrong on which cars would survive. Angus Motors and Ruby Motors at 400 and 404 Selby sold such ill-fated cars as the Graham, Auburn, and Chandler.

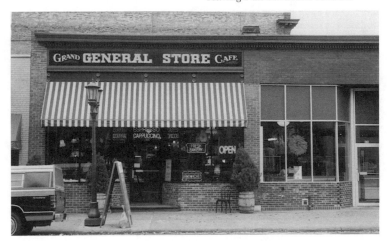

The old Crocus Hill Market, now the Grand General Store and Cafe. (David Lanegran photo.)

Grocery stores were the mainstay of the avenue almost from its beginning. Every block had a grocery of some sort, often a tiny shop in one room of an apartment. Most of the grocery stores offered an extraordinary level of service to their customers.

The day would begin for the Crocus Hill Market and the Grand Avenue Grocery with the ringing of dozens of telephones. Customers were calling in their orders for home delivery later that day. Clerks would fill the orders from the high shelves, riding a rolling ladder to reach the provisions and grasping canned goods with a claw device mounted on the end of a long pole. Some of the cashier's cages were up on the balconies. When payments were made, the clerks would put the money in a little basket, yank on a cord and the money would go rattling up to the balcony. In a few minutes the basket would return with the change.

Some stores had meat markets with sawdust on the floor. When orders were ready, they would be packed into collapsible wooden boxes and loaded onto the trucks for delivery. The Grand Avenue Market trucks had roofs but the sides were open with rolled up curtains that could be lowered in bad weather. The bed of the truck sloped toward the center so a box of groceries would not be thrown off if the truck rounded a curve at too great a speed. Once at the customer's home, the delivery man would carry the groceries into the kitchen and unload them onto the counter or table. If a customer needed something in a hurry for a special dinner party, delivery in an hour was available.

Neighborhood housewives had their favorite clerks, one in groceries and the other in meats. If produce was wilted or the meat tough, they were quick to complain. As the clerks knew all of the customers, the complaints could gen-

The Piggly-Wiggly store on Grand (left), about 1925. The Piggly-Wiggly store and Twin City Meat Market (right), about 1923 to 1926, shows the turnstyle that so delighted neighborhood children. (Photos courtesy of the Minnesota Historical Society.)

erally be negotiated with promises to improve the service and the selection. Ed Wall, the owner of the Grand Avenue Grocery, was known as a lady's man. He wore a homburg hat and camel's-hair coat and drove a fancy convertible car.

Though the Crocus Hill Market and the Grand Avenue Grocery were favorites with Crocus Hill housewives, there were other substantial grocery stores on the street. For a time Piggly Wiggly had three stores on Grand: one at Dale, one near Milton and another near Fairview. These stores were among the first to offer self-service and introduced the first turnstile that anyone in the neighborhood had seen before. Installed at the entrance to the store, the wooden turnstile was an object of curiosity and interest, particularly for the neighborhood children who made many visits to the store just to walk through the device. Klein's was a discount supermarket across the street from the Grand Avenue Grocery. Clerks from the Grand Avenue Grocery, in their distinctive green smocks, could often be seen pushing shopping carts in Klein's, buying groceries for resale at higher prices across the street.

Typical of the smaller, neighborhood grocery stores was The Corner Grocery at 1158 Grand Avenue run for thirty-five years by Rose and Isadore Yugend. Rose had immigrated from Russia, and Isadore was from Poland. They first lived in the Fourteenth Street neighborhood near Mechanic Arts High School. Rose worked in a sweater factory, and Isadore painted cars for the Northern Pacific Railroad. They saved their money and, in 1937, bought the store on Grand Avenue from Morris Yblonsky, reasoning, as Rose told their son Jerome, that "they would never go hungry if they had a grocery store." Yblonsky continued to live in an apartment upstairs. Isadore's middle name was Harry. Everyone with whom they did business called him Harry, and he liked that.

Because they did not own a car, the Yugends had to find a place to live near their new business. With Rose's brother and sister-in-law, Harry bought a duplex a few blocks from the store, at 1143 Goodrich, for $7,500. The four Yugends lived upstairs, and the brother and his family occupied the downstairs unit.

With no help other than that provided by their two children, Harry and Rose kept the store open seven days a week, staying open on weekdays and Saturdays from 8:00 in the morning until 9:00 P.M., and opening from 9:00 A.M. to 6:00 P.M. on Sundays. Groceries were delivered to customers within an approximate six-block radius of the store. When a customer phoned in an order, Yugend and his son would pack the groceries in boxes, put the boxes under their arms and walk to their customer's homes. Many of the phone orders came from the residents of four nearby apartment buildings at numbers 1160, 1168, 1180 and 1186 Grand. Yugend's daughter, Sylviette, would help her mother wait on customers.

The Yugend family, about 1946. From left to right: Sylviette, Harry, Rose, and Jerome. (Photo courtesy of Jerome Yugend.)

According to Jerome, the Yugends never had a checking account and never made a purchase until they had accumulated the money to pay for it. Payments that had to be mailed were paid with a postal money order. Every month, his mother would get on the trolley and ride downtown to pay the gas and electric bills in cash. Even when their children were in college, Jerome remembers his mother taking money out of the grocery store cash register to give him to pay his tuition at the University of Minnesota.

The Grand Avenue streetcar stopped at the corner in front of the store, and people getting off the car would come in to visit. Conversations buzzed constantly between customers, salesmen, and passers-by who wanted to visit. Jerome remembers people sitting on the counter talking, moving off so his father could take care of a customer, and then sitting back down to resume the conversation. One of the regular visitors was the chairman of the board of the Great Northern Railroad. He would get off the streetcar in front of the store on his way home from work and come in for a chat with Harry.

The store hours the Yugends maintained represented a personal sacrifice on their part; they could only attend the Temple of Aaron Synagogue infrequently. Sylviette remembers that, after sundown on Fridays, Rose would light the Sabbath candles at the store and recite the blessings of thankfulness. The store was the Yugend's life, and their customers were their best friends. Children coming home from

Lacher Drug Store at 1820 Grand in 1938. (Photo courtesy of Abbott Paint.)

school stopped for penny candy. Pranksters would call on the telephone with the question, "Are you on the streetcar line?" When Yugend would reply that he was, the caller would gleefully respond with, "You'd better get off. There's a streetcar coming," and hang up.

Toward the end of his career as a grocer, Yugend ordered an automobile. Somehow his frugal wife, Rose, got wind of it and immediately canceled the order.[6]

Besides the grocery stores, the drugstores were the other major commercial presence on Grand Avenue. Of the nine intersections between Dale and Lexington, eight had drugstores on one of their corners in 1930s. Joe at the Grandendale drug store was reputed to make the best malted milks. Mr. Wesley St. Clair at St. Alben's Street is remembered as being a very dignified gentleman with a stiff high collar and a pince-nez. Gustav Dickman ran the pharmacy at Avon and allowed the children to call him "Gussie." A Mr. Lietzow ran Conger's at Grotto, Harry Shapiro was at Chatsworth, Mr. Brotchner at Milton, Mr. Dietz at Oxford, and Mr. Treacy at Lexington.

Like the grocery stores, the drugstores were family-run businesses. The owners themselves usually came out to wait on customers, sell candy to the children (who took forever deciding what to buy), make sodas and to give out free glasses of water.

Prohibition undoubtedly helped keep the many drug-stores on Grand Avenue in business. Vicenta Donnelly Scar-lett remembers riding in the family car down Grand Avenue as a girl when her family made a stop at one of the drug-stores. Vicenta commented that the store was so small she wondered how it could stay in business. Her mother replied that she needn't be concerned as the owner was a bootlegger and was, therefore, doing very well.

The Volstead Act of 1920, authored by Minnesota Congressman Andrew Volstead, prohibited the sale and manufacture of alcohol with certain exceptions. One of those exceptions was an allotment of alcohol, of about seven gal-lons a year, made to doctors and dentists. Drugstores were the dispensers of this alcohol to the doctors, who were allowed to prescribe it for their patients, presumably for med-ical reasons.

Cooperative local doctors wrote prescriptions for al-cohol for their patients and friends. These prescriptions were filled at the drugstores on Grand. The prescriptions were generous, calling for a full gallon of alcohol, which was sent home in cans made for that purpose, called "alcohol cans." More often than not, the alcohol cans were filled with boot-leg liquor, sold under the labels of the regular drugstore alco-hol. Once home, the "medicinal" alcohol was used to spike drinks and enliven a draught of near beer. Alcohol was even dispensed by a local dairy, which brought it around to cus-tomers with the daily delivery of milk.

The dispensing of illegal alcohol became a major busi-ness on Grand Avenue during the years of prohibition. Since the residents of the neighborhood (and most other people in St. Paul) had no intention of cutting out their evening cock-tails after the passage of the Volstead Act, illegal stills sprang up throughout eastern Minnesota. One of these stills could produce a gallon of liquor for about fifty cents that, thanks to prohibition, sold for a minimum of five dollars. A hundred-gallon still could be set up for five hundred dollars, and it would pay for itself in a week. The largest still in a region encompassing the Dakotas, Minnesota, and Wisconsin, was located about three miles east of Dodge, Minnesota. The still produced 1,500 gallons of alcohol daily.[7]

This was a vast quantity of moonshine, and, while much of it was shipped east to Chicago, a large proportion flowed into the Twin Cities and onto Grand Avenue. One of the distributors of this illegal alcohol on Grand Avenue was the Belco Company, also known as the Radio Girl Perfume Company at 776 Grand. This company appeared to use vast quantities of alcohol in its manufacturing. Large tank trucks would discharge cargo in the alley at the back of the building while the only product appearing to go out of the front were tiny ten cent vials of Radio Girl Perfume. Sometimes store officials would hand out the vials to school children walking home. One remembers giving the vial to her mother who took one sniff and, with a grimace, threw it into the trash.

Another distributor of illegal alcohol was Malarky's Candy and Bakery. Lawrence Platt remembers that the owner, Mr. Malarky, would give the children free candy or a stale doughnut to get rid of them, telling them to, "Go on home and tell yer mother she's callin' ya." The children thought something unusual must be going on in a store with stale candy on nearly empty shelves. Platt's suspicions were confirmed when he asked his father for a dime for candy in the presence of his young uncle and a friend. As Platt tells it, "The young men just about knocked themselves out laughing. 'Not goin' to Malarky's are ya?' Then more guffaws. Between laughs I gathered that Malarky's was a speakeasy downstairs." The neighborhood youth spent some time on their stomachs looking in the basement windows at Malarky's, hoping to see a drunken orgy, but all they saw were tables with checked tablecloths, chairs, and a bar.[8]

For many small business people, too small to be listed in the city directory or located elsewhere in the city, Grand was the locale where they found their clients, promoted and performed their services. Among the businesses that plied their trade on the street was the vegetable man who made rounds of the streets and alleys in the summer, ringing his bell and calling out the names of the vegetables he had for sale. Rag men drove rickety wagons down the alleys looking for rags and scrap metal they could recycle.

The ice man from the Citizens Ice and Fuel Company delivered ice in the winter with a horse and sleigh and wore a leather apron on his back with a fold at the bottom that formed a trough so melting ice would not drip on the kitchen floors of his customers. Ice was ordered by placing a card in the house window with the number (25, 50, 75, or 100) at the top of the card indicating the amount of ice the housewife wanted delivered. The ice man would split the big blocks into the desired size, hook tongs into the chunk, hoist it onto his shoulder and carry it into the kitchen where he put it into the ice box. In summer, groups of children followed the ice man to beg slivers of ice from him. In winter, they hitched rides behind his sleigh, skidding along on the soles of their boots. Platt, who grew up at 849 Osceola, three blocks south of Grand Avenue, remembers, "The driver would pretend not to notice for a block or two and then would shoo the riders off."

The milk delivery men made daily visits, driving a horse-drawn wagon in the early 1930s. The horses knew the routes, stopping automatically at each house and only became confused when new customers were added and others dropped. The milkmen wore white pinstriped coveralls and brown canvas aprons fastened with buckles that clinked when they walked. The rattling of the glass bottles in the sectioned metal baskets was the first sound heard on the streets in the mornings.

Platt remembers five dairies that made stops on Grand Avenue and neighboring streets, including the Sanitary Farm Dairy, Minnesota Milk, Schroeder Cream Top, and "some company that featured Golden Guernsey unpasteurized milk, which had a lot of appeal to the natural food zealots of the day until raw milk was revealed as a major source of tuberculosis."

Coal was also delivered down Grand Avenue by horse and wagon. Every house had a coal chute leading to the basement. Men carried up to 100 pounds of coal in baskets on their shoulders from the wagon to the house, dumping it down the chute into the basement until two or three tons had been accumulated.

Five friends in the neighborhood in 1933. From left to right: Alden Dean, Harriet Stringer (Chapman), Laura Dean (Platt), Mary Stringer (Wilson), and Winter (Buddy) Dean. (Photo courtesy of Mary Wilson.)

In summer, children in the Grand Avenue neighborhood were entertained by a balloon man, three popcorn men, and a roving photographer with a brightly painted goat cart. For twenty-five cents, the photographer would take a picture of a child seated in the wagon behind the patient goat. The three popcorn men were Pete, George, and Bill—rivals who,

Harriet Stringer (Chapman) and her sister Mary Stringer (Wilson) photographed in a goat cart in 1929. (Photo courtesy of Mary Wilson.)

though fierce competitors, managed to avoid each other on the neighboring streets. Pete's wagon had signs on the front and back. The sign in front read, "Here comes Pete" while the sign on the back read, "There goes Pete."

There was even an Italian hurdy-gurdy with a live red-capped monkey. The monkey would pretend to lift the girls' skirts and then go into a fit of crazy antics, an act boys thought hilarious but was universally frowned on by parents.

Grace Granzberg, who has lived at 1053 Fairmount since 1925, remembers the black-habited Little Sisters of the Poor who drove a horse-drawn, open, black wagon down Grand Avenue on regular rounds to pick up day-old bread from Olson's bakery where Wuollet's Bakery stands now.

Of all the business people on the street, the chimney sweeps were perhaps the most colorful. Chief among the sweeps was a man known to the neighborhood as "Slunky" Norton. His real name was L.A. Stolpp, and he maintained two offices, one downtown and another at 1322 Grand Avenue. Slunky wore a black silk top hat and a dirty cut-away coat. Usually a crowd of children followed him down the street. He carried a sooty burlap bag full of swabs and brushes, and, once on the ridgepole of a house, before descending the chimney, he would blow a blast on a bugle that could be heard throughout the neighborhood.

Slunky had a Christmas sideline. Laura Platt remembers that he would hire himself out as a Santa Claus at Christmas parties for children at the big houses in the neighborhood and at the appropriate moment, dressed in a red Santa suit, would come crashing down the chimney and out the fireplace opening, to the astonishment and delight of his youthful audience.

A major event of the 1920s was the opening of the Oxford Theater, one block east of Lexington Avenue on Grand across the street from the Oxford Club. The neighborhood was full of young families, eager to participate in this new form of entertainment. The theater seated 1,200 people, and, when it was built, it was the largest neighborhood theater in St. Paul. The interior decoration of the theater was described by the *St. Paul Pioneer Press* as being in "a modern Italian decorative style." The first films shown were silent, starring such greats as Clara Bow, Rudolf Valentino, the Barrymores, and Felix the Cat. The drama and antics were enlivened with organ accompaniment on a Barton pipe organ played by Alfred F. Becker.

Among the first features offered by the new theater were: *The Old Nest*, a domestic drama by *Saturday Evening*

Post author Rupert Hughes; *The Sting of the Lash,* with actress Pauline Frederick; and *Dangerous Curve Ahead*, starring Helene Chadwick and Richard Dix. Mack Sennett's comedy, *Down on the Farm*, was also shown. A Saturday film for children starring Pearl White, Ruth Roland, and Pauline Frederick was *Perils of Pauline*. Mary E. Hoffman remembered *Casey of the Coast Guard* as one of the best films. Theater manager George W. Granstrom promised patrons the "biggest and cleanest pictures obtainable." Admission was thirty cents for adults and eleven cents for children under twelve.[9]

During the summer, the theater was opened up every morning to air it out. While it was open, Mary and other neighborhood children would go in and produce little plays on the empty stage. When sound was added to the films, the Oxford installed the appropriate equipment and became a "second run" theater. Films had their first showing in the downtown theaters and, after a few weeks, reappeared at the Oxford.[10]

In 1929, the Oxford was acquired by the Finkelstein and Ruben firm, which closed it for remodeling. When it reopened as the Uptown Theater on April 22, the newspaper called it "one of the showplaces of the city as well as a temple of amusement which ranks with any in the largest cities of the country."

The name change to "Uptown" was significant as it reflected how the residents of Grand Avenue thought of themselves. The Grand Avenue neighborhood was not just another section of St. Paul in the eyes of its residents. Instead, the people saw their area as a distinctive and identifiable area of the city, second only to the "downtown"—the central business district.

The Uptown remodeling was designed by Mark A. Wright in a style identified by the paper as "Italian Renaissance with a hint of Turkish design in the Moorish arches." The walls of rough, hand-troweled plaster were punctuated with small "Juliet" balconies, complete with iron rails and flower boxes with artificial flowers, all subtly lit from within. At the top of the walls, red tiles simulated the edge of a Mediterranean roof, and, above them, the curved deep-blue ceiling glimmered with hundreds of tiny lights, like stars in a midnight sky. Among the occasional patrons of the Uptown theater was John Dillinger, who came from his apartment at the corner of Lincoln and Lexington. He was said to have always occupied an aisle seat with quick access to an exit.

The Saturday matinee cost ten cents, and most of the

children in the neighborhood attended regularly, seeing for their dime a cartoon (Popeye, Betty Boop, Mickey Mouse) then a short comedy with Pete Smith or Laurel and Hardy. Next came an episode of a serial and finally a feature film, especially selected for the Saturday crowd. Cowboys and Indians chased each other across the screen throughout the afternoon while the audience whooped and hollered for their favorites. Platt remembers the head usher, "in a uniform so splendid that they wouldn't have had to pay me a cent if I could wear it— a magnificent raiment of powder and royal blue with maroon trim, garnet studs in the stiff shirt and a cape."

Refreshments for the Saturday matinee crowd came from Myrtle Brack's rental library at 1050 Grand Avenue. Besides renting books, Myrtle sold bags of popcorn with red-skin peanuts in it. She is remembered by her former customers as a person who was very nice to children.

For the children and youth growing up in the Grand Avenue neighborhood in the first four decades of the century, the street was more than a transportation corridor—it was social space. Grand was where they met their friends, observed strangers and tried to figure out how the world around them was organized.

Bob McLeod remembers that the families living on the west end of Grand were large, many with eight to ten children. They played sports together, attended the Immaculate Heart of Mary and St. Luke's schools, held soap-box derbys in the alley. In the summer, they held carnivals "and never thought twice about being in other people's yards." The doors to the houses were seldom locked. Just as the streets around a Mexican plaza become the living room of the village, Grand Avenue became the stage on which many small human dramas were acted out.

The protagonist of one of these dramas was a man named Dick who spent much of his life hanging around the Grandendale Drug Store in the 1930s. Dick had a slight hump on his back and was mildly retarded, but he knew trolley cars. Dick kept an exact record in his head of the daily comings and goings of the streetcars. He knew which were on schedule, which were late, where stalled cars were, horses down, and dogs run over. To find out if a trolley had already gone by, a passenger had only to ask Dick as he knew everything that was happening with the trolley. The motormen let him ride free out to the end of the line at Cretin where the cars switched back to begin their return trip down Grand.

Notes

1. James Taylor Dunn, *Grand Avenue in the Early 1900s*, Reprints of *Grand Gazette* articles.

2. Dunn.

3. Lemon, p. 51.

4. Matters, *Grand Avenue Promenade*.

5. Lawrence Platt, *Grand Gazette* (St. Paul, Minnesota, April, 1992).

6. Interview by Billie Young with Jerome Yugend, June 8, 1995. Sylviette remembers that Rose's antipathy to buying an automobile was based, not on frugality, but on their devotion to their children. She writes, "To Rose and Harry the most important things in life were their children, Jerome and Sylviette, and their education. To avoid their children from being distracted by material things, like an automobile, they sacrificed their own personal gratification by doing without that luxury. A car meant that their children would spend less time studying and more time doing things that might lower their grade point level. Both graduated with honors from the University of Minnesota."

7. The economic possibilities presented by Prohibition were not lost on many Minnesotans, particularly on those for whom the consumption of alcohol had cultural origins. In the city of New Ulm, with its predominately German population, forty percent of the city's square blocks contained at least one illegal still.

8. Interview by Billie Young with Lawrence Platt, November 25, 1994. Platt lived in the Grand Avenue neighborhood for over sixty years and wrote an engaging column of reminiscences for the *Grand Gazette* entitled, "That Was Then." Many of the incidents from the 1930s and 1940s are taken from his writings and recollections.

9. Dunn, *Grand Gazette*, August 1976. See also *St. Paul Dispatch*, November 18, 1921, Mary Hoffman, *Grand Gazette*, September 1976.

10. Platt, *Grand Gazette*, October 1991.

The Benner Lunch Box
Company at 750 Grand
about 1925. (Photo courtesy
of the Minnesota Historical
Society.)

Store building at 1680
Grand, ca. 1910. (Photo
courtesy of the Minnesota
Historical Society.)

4

Glamorous Gangsters on Grand

THE ENACTMENT OF PROHIBITION in 1920 and a city government controlled by a tight little group of political bosses led to St. Paul's national reputation as the safe haven for gangsters, many of whom spent time on and around Grand Avenue. For the first twenty-five years of the century, the city was run by an especially unsavory trio. They were Richard O'Connor, head of the Democratic Party in St. Paul and known as "The Cardinal"; his brother John J. O'Connor, police chief; and a speakeasy owner with a criminal record known as Dapper Danny Hogan.

These three negotiated a clearly understood agreement with criminals that, if they would keep a steady flow of money coming into the pockets of police and city officials, the police would, in return, look the other way where criminal activity was concerned. When Hogan was killed in 1928 by a car bomb, his role was taken over by Harry "Dutch" Sawyer, who created an even more complex citywide organization of politicians, police, weapons salesmen, bootleggers, money launderers, businessmen, and lawyers who provided services to criminals. Many levels of government and private enterprise were involved, as well as many of St. Paul's leading citizens. The police department, city council, and judges were all a part of a system that shared in the profits from crime and protected the criminals.

The "O'Connor system" worked like this: crooks coming into St. Paul had to check in with Dapper Danny on

45

Officer Mike Cullen and his horse, Eleanor Patch, which Cullen claimed was the granddaughter of Dan Patch of harness racing fame. Cullen and Eleanor Patch patrolled Grand Avenue in the early 1900s. The horse was stabled behind the Cullen home at 197 South Lexington. (Photo courtesy of Elberta Matters.)

their arrival in town, either at his speakeasy, the Green Lantern Cafe at 545½ Wabasha Street, or else at the Hollyhocks Club at 1590 South Mississippi River Boulevard. To avoid being bothered by the police, the outlaws had to make substantial protection payments regularly, and they could not commit crimes within the city limits of St. Paul.

For a time, the O'Connor system did control crime in St. Paul, but it also turned the city into a staging area for bank robberies and murders throughout the region. It mattered little to O'Connor that the gangsters he protected in St. Paul robbed banks in the Dakotas and in rural Minnesota, cracked safes in Iowa and kidnapped citizens in other cities. The O'Connor system fostered a climate in St. Paul where bootlegging, prostitution, extortion, and gambling flourished, and public officials—from policemen to judges—were corrupted.

Word of St. Paul's "arrangement" spread rapidly throughout the country's underworld, and soon the most notorious of national crime figures became common sights on the streets of St. Paul. The Grand Avenue neighborhood was among the most popular with national crime figures. John Dillinger, members of the Barker-Karpis gang, Edna "The Kissing Bandit" Murray, Frank "Jelly" Nash, Verne "Kansas City Massacre" Miller frequented the area. Residents learned to recognize some of the individuals on the streets, and, because of the way their exploits had been written up in the popular press, they were considered glamorous characters by children. The Hollyhocks Club was frequented by the business and social leadership of the city, who found it exciting to dine in the company of notorious criminals whose likenesses were featured in the *True Crime* magazines. An editorial writer for the *St. Paul Dispatch* lamented, "Why is St. Paul a happy hunting ground for the nation's worst gangsters and crooks?" He answered his own question, adding that they were "safer from capture here than in any other city."[1]

John Dillinger. (FBI photo.)

The roots of crime and civic corruption were found in the prohibition of alcohol. Bootlegging—the making and selling of illegal liquor—became so profitable that small-time crooks quickly became multimillionaires and used their gains to buy political power. Men like Harry Sawyer and Leon Gleckman bought off juries and judges, paid bribes to policemen to overlook criminal behavior and became the bosses—the Al Capones of St. Paul.

The nationally famous criminals who made St. Paul (and in many cases Grand Avenue) their headquarters were all initiated into crime through the illegal liquor trade. Though they later moved on into bank robbery, kidnapping, and murder, bootlegging was the platform from which they launched their activities. Annual profits from a single bootleg operation could run into the millions of dollars. A large majority of the population ignored the law and either made their own booze or bought illegal liquor from others. St. Paul Police Chief Michael Gebhardt estimated that seventy-five percent of St. Paul citizens were distilling moonshine. A major brewery, Schmidt, while it produced root beer and near-beer during prohibition, also made illicit alcohol for sale in speakeasies.[2]

The pervasiveness of illegal activity in St. Paul among all levels of society is illustrated by a column written by Gary Hiebert in the *St. Paul Dispatch* in which he told the story of a "Mr. Lucky," who had been the "gentleman supplier of liquor for the city's gentlemen" during Prohibition. Mr. Lucky, who did not want his real name revealed, had been paid $1,500 a trip for rum runs to Canada, where he loaded up on alcoholic beverages for the city's social and business elite. His customers were "the social register of St. Paul in that raw time of prohibition when the city stood on the threshold of its most infamous label, 'crime center of the nation.'"

Mr. Lucky was among the ten percent of the local purveyors of illegal alcohol who managed to remain independent and avoid control by the gangsters. Nevertheless, he did not escape unscathed; his mother was tortured, and his brother was thrown out of a moving gangster's car in front of the St. Paul Cathedral.

Mr. Lucky's career began when he was recruited by a prominent member of St. Paul's business establishment to procure liquor for him and his friends from Canada. Border guards and customs officials were cooperative so long as they were paid their fee of $2.00 per case. However, Mr. Lucky's many trips to Canada did not go unnoticed by the crooks of St. Paul who resented the fact that he was cutting into their profits from the illegal sale of alcohol. One night they summoned him to the Ryan Hotel and gave him the choice of quitting, joining them or being killed. He quit. But then the local banker called him and said, "We want you to keep on. We'll get you protection. We'll fix it so the police pass the word to the mob to leave you alone."

Mr. Lucky related that he "went up to police headquarters and talked to a certain big shot, and he promised nothing would happen to me. I guess he kept his word, but they got to my mother and brother. I decided to quit and I was stuck with $11,000 worth of liquor. One of St. Paul's most prominent citizens arranged to have me deliver it to his garage in the dead of night. He lived on Summit Avenue. He met me and paid—never counted the cases." Mr. Lucky eventually went to Europe for a time to escape retribution from the gangsters.[3]

The widespread disregard for the law by so many citizens, and the existence of the O'Connor system, made St. Paul a magnet for national crime figures seeking safe cities. The alliance between the St. Paul police, who tipped off the gangsters in advance of staged raids, and the criminals was the foundation on which gangs like the Barker-Karpis group could stage their crime waves of the 1930s.

One of the hideouts of the Barker-Karpis gang was the Edgecumbe Court Apartments at the northeast corner of Osceola Avenue and Lexington, four blocks south of Grand Avenue. The building was like a dormitory for bank robbers. Others who lived there were Frank "Jelly" Nash, Verne Miller, Arthur "Doc" Barker, Volney "Curly" Davis, Edna "the Kissing Bandit" Murray, and two train robbers—Francis

L. "Jimmy" Keating and Tommy Holden. Lester "Baby-face Nelson" Gillis was a frequent visitor.

From the relative safety of the Edgcombe Court, the bandits conducted their raids on banks in rural Minnesota and as far south as Texas. In 1932 , twenty-one percent of all bank holdups in the United States occurred in Minnesota and robbers struck five North Dakota banks in one thirteen day period.[4]

The Edgcombe was not the only area hang-out of gang members. Charles and Paula Harmon, members of the Barker-Karpis gang, lived at the Lincoln Oaks apartments at 572 Lincoln, one block south of Grand. Harmon was shot following the robbery of the Kraft State Bank of Menomonie, Wisconsin.

Holden and Keating, with their wives, later moved into apartments in the Summit-Dale building at 616 Summit Avenue. Keating had an elaborate wardrobe and would take five expensive suits at a time to be pressed at Zolly Vetloff's dry cleaners at 2166 Grand.[5] Holden's wife, Lillian, ordered a baby grand piano and a fur coat. Both couples ate frequently at the French Cafe at 38 South Dale Street where the La Cucaracha restaurant is today.

The robbery of the Third Northwestern National Bank in Minneapolis was planned at the Annbee Arms apartments at 928 Grand Avenue by a member of the Barker-Karpis gang, machine gunner Larry DeVols. DeVols was a murderer who had blown up almost forty safes and was involved in the killing of two police officers in a Minneapolis bank holdup.[6]

Another residence of Ma Barker's gang in St. Paul was at 1290 Grand where three apartments were rented. Unaccountably, the gang neglected to have a telephone installed. The purpose of the telephone was to receive tips from the St. Paul police when they were planning a raid. In March 1933, Harry Sawyer of the Green Lantern Saloon heard from the St. Paul police that 1290 Grand was about to be raided. Since the gang had not yet had a phone installed, Sawyer sent his wife Gladys to alert them. The gang members all packed their suitcases and walked out the door past three policemen on the sidewalk who postponed their raid until all the gang members had had a chance to flee.

The O'Connor system, which supposedly kept crime out of the city of St. Paul, broke down when Fred Barker and Alvin Karpis, along with Jack Pfeifer, hatched a plot at the Hollyhocks Club to kidnap William Hamm, Jr., the president of St. Paul's Hamm Brewing Company. The young Hamm was snatched on June 15, 1933, as he was walking home for lunch. The ransom demand was for $100,000. The man chosen as the negotiator between the Hamm family and the kidnappers was William Dunn who lived at 1916 Summit Avenue and was an employee of the brewery. The choice of Dunn clearly illustrated the blurred line between legal and illegal activity in the city at that time, for Dunn was also the contact man between the underworld and the St. Paul police department and collected for Leon Gleckman, the man who controlled gambling in St. Paul.

The first ransom demand in the kidnapping was made to Dunn at his office in the brewery. The second demand was a note left at Clarence J. Thomas' Rosedale Pharmacy at 1941 Grand Avenue. A caller on the phone directed a clerk to where the note had been left and instructed him to deliver it to Dunn's house around the corner. On June 17, the ransom money was paid at a site near Pine City, and Hamm was released unharmed.

The Dale Apartments at 628 Grand Avenue were the site of the planning for the next kidnapping. Members of the Barker-Karpis gang met in the living room of apartment 103 to plan the abduction and ransom of Edward Bremer of the Jacob Schmidt Brewing Company. Bremer had taken his daughter, Betty, to the Summit School at 1150 Goodrich Avenue when he stopped at the intersection of Goodrich and Lexington. Before he could start up again, his car was blocked, and he was taken by Barker, Karpis, and two others who hit him over the head when he struggled.

The Grand Avenue neighborhood was again the center of the action. The go-between selected by the kidnappers to receive their ransom demands was Walter W. Magee, who lived at 1295 Lincoln Avenue. A ransom note was also delivered in a bottle, thrown through the glass door of the home of Bremer's family physician, Dr. Henry T. Nippert at 706 Lincoln Avenue.[7] Bremer was released after twenty-one days in captivity and a ransom of $200,000 had been paid.

After the two kidnappings, public opinion began to turn against the city administration of St. Paul for its policy of tolerance to national crime figures. Howard Kahn, the fearless editor of the *St. Paul Daily News*, lambasted public officials with scathing editorials about crime in the city. Finally, a blue ribbon committee was appointed to sit as the Ramsey County Grand Jury to investigate the charges of collusion with criminals among law enforcement officials.

On March 31, 1934, the long-awaited report was broadcast on the noon radio news that there was "no justification for any charges that an excess of crime exists here." The timing was extraordinary, for that was the very day on which occurred the most dramatic gangster shoot out in the history of St. Paul and the Grand Avenue neighborhood.

John Dillinger, the most wanted man in America, and his girlfriend Evelyn "Billie" Frechette had taken an apartment in the Lincoln Court Apartments at 93-95 Lexington Parkway using the name of Mr. and Mrs. Carl P. Hellman. Homer Van Meter, a partner of Dillinger's and a much-wanted gangster, was a frequent visitor.

On the morning of March 31, two FBI agents and a St. Paul policeman went to the apartment building to investigate a tip from the building owner that the residents were behaving in a suspicious manner. They kept the blinds pulled down most of the day, she reported, and only came and went by the back door. The policeman knocked at the door and Evelyn answered. The police officer asked to speak to Carl Hellman.

"Carl who?" asked Billie, forgetting Dillinger's alias. She turned the officer away and closed the door.

At that moment Van Meter drove up to the apartment building and walked into the hallway. Although he quickly claimed to be a soap salesman, the FBI men recognized him and gunfire broke out. Dillinger fired his machine gun through a crack in the apartment door and Van Meter fired from the hallway. The gunfight spilled out into the street with Dillinger brandishing his automatic weapon in the alley while Evelyn backed their car out of the garage. In the hail of bullets the three gangsters got away, but Dillinger had been shot in the leg.

The O'Connor era was coming to an end. Under public safety commissioner H.E. " Ned" Warren of Grand Avenue fame, wiretaps exposed the corruption of police inspectors openly soliciting bribes from gambling operations in the basement of St. Paul's Hamm Building. Prohibition was repealed and St. Paul citizens wanted a change. A reform mayor, Mark Gehan, was elected.

Though the policemen dodging bullets could not know it at the time, they were nearing the end of an era. Soon more lethal bullets would be flying, and the nation would forget its preoccupation with Prohibition and gangsters in the tumult of World War II. The war years and their aftermath were to bring profound changes to St. Paul and a disastrous decline to the Grand Avenue neighborhood from which it would not recover for almost thirty years.

Notes

1. Steve Thayer, "Crime," *Minneapolis Star Tribune*, June 13, 1991, p. 3E. See also Paul Maccabee, "John Dillinger Slept Here," *Mpls/St. Paul Magazine*, August 1995, p. 48, and *Highland Villager*, August 30, 1995, p. 27.

2. Paul Maccabee, *John Dillinger Slept Here* (St. Paul, Minnesota Historical Society Press, 1995), p. 25.

3. Gary Hiebert, "Oliver Towne Column," *St. Paul Dispatch*, January 24, 1961.

4. Maccabee, p. 78.

5. Maccabee, p. 89.

6. Maccabee, p.122.

7. Maccabee, p. 197.

Grand and Fairview in 1932, looking north on Fairview. (Photo courtesy the Minnesota Historical Society.)

5

What the Great War Did to Grand

THE MOST IMMEDIATE EFFECT of World War II on the Grand Avenue neighborhood was to create a housing shortage. Margaret Nath remembers living on the second floor at 669 Grand Avenue in 1940 and 1941. She shared a single sleeping room with another woman and used the bathroom at the end of the hall. Their bathroom was shared with two others, a man in a studio apartment and another woman, also in a single sleeping room. Margaret rode the trolley to downtown St. Paul to her job at the Tri-State Telephone Company, the precursor to Northwest Bell and US West.

The construction industry had been drafted during World War II, and, as a result, few new buildings were built from 1942 through 1946. People working in the war effort crowded into the cities to take rooms and apartments wherever they were available. The large older homes of the Hill district and Grand Avenue were prime candidates for subdivision. Apartments were carved out of attics and basements. Large closets were converted to small kitchens for one room apartments. Single room apartments with shared baths were common. Both occupants and the absentee landlords engaged in the conversion of single-family houses into multiple-family units. Some of the conversions were carefully done, but most were carried out with whatever materials and labor were available at the time. There was a war on, and people needed shelter. Many of the conversions were in violation of the zoning regulations, but few complained and the city government ignored the violations.

The impact of the wartime housing shortage was felt most keenly in the neighborhoods north of Summit Avenue and along the bluff itself. The largest homes in the area were converted into dozens of sleeping rooms and small apartments. The high densities hastened the deterioration of the buildings. Absentee landlords determined they could maximize return on their investment by not putting any more money in their buildings and, instead, waited for a new land use to develop, which would convert the worn-out housing to another profitable use. Although there were a few exceptions, the entire area north of Summit to University Avenue began an obvious downward spiral.

After the war, residents gradually lost confidence in the future of the neighborhood. After generations of being the elite address in St. Paul, the east end of Summit Avenue began to look seedy. Mansions on Summit and Portland, built like fortresses, their interiors museums of old world craftsmanship, were closed up, subdivided into apartments, abandoned, torn down or given to the Catholic Church.

The years of World War II and those immediately following were not kind to the Twin Cities' extensive streetcar network. Ridership on the cars had been dropping steadily from the high of 226 million passengers reached in 1922. In 1932, only 113 million passengers put tokens in the box, and, by 1940, ridership had dropped to 104 million passengers. The surge in automobile ownership after the war hastened the decline. Auto registrations in the Twin Cities increased by fifty-eight percent between 1947 and 1950—twenty times the rate of increase during the previous two decades.

In 1945, in an attempt to stimulate public support for the streetcars, a new car was designed called the President's Conference Car. This new car was streamlined, sleek and quiet with a wide center door that made it easier for passengers to step in and out of the car. One hundred and forty President's Conference Cars were built in St. Paul and put into service on lines in the Twin Cities.

Before the impact of the new cars could be fully assessed, the Twin City Rapid Transit company suffered another blow. The company, which had been highly successful and conservatively managed, attracted the attention of a New York stockholder named Charles Green. In 1949 Green, with the assistance of Fred A. Ossanna, a Twin Cities attorney with reputed connections to St. Paul's underworld leaders, waged a proxy fight and won control of the company. With Green and Ossanna in charge, the maintenance on the cars (which had been kept in pristine condition) was cut

back, routes were closed, and fares raised. Thousands of citizens were left to freeze on street corners in long waits for
cars during Minnesota's sub-zero winter weather. More than
twenty-five percent of the staff were released. Outraged citizen groups complained to the State Railroad and Warehouse
Commission, which issued a temporary restraining order
against closing any more lines without a public hearing.

Then, in 1950, Green and Ossanna had a falling out,
and Green was ousted from the company's management.
Ossanna took control, and the shutting down of the streetcar lines accelerated. Convinced that buses were the urban
transportation mode of the future, Ossanna went to General
Motors in Detroit with funds to purchase twenty-five new
diesel buses—all that he could afford. Roger Kyes, of General
Motors, who would later become the Assistant Secretary of
Defense in the Eisenhower administration, offered the
astounded Ossanna terms for 525 buses.

That was the final and fatal blow for the streetcars.
The beautifully crafted President's Conference Cars were
sold for $395, a fraction of their value. Some went to the
cities of Newark, Cleveland, and Mexico City, where they
were seen in use years later. Other cars were used for sheds,
construction shacks, and camp mess halls. Those that were
not sold were burned. On October 31, 1953, the last streetcar operated on the streets of St. Paul. It was the end of what
had been one of the world's best electric railway systems.
Collier's Weekly, in September 1951, published an article
entitled, "How Mobsters Grabbed a City's Transit Line." On

The Grand Avenue bus that
replaced the last streetcars.
(Photo by Elberta Matters.)

Grand Avenue, the streetcar tracks were buried under asphalt, and bus signs replaced the old streetcar stops.[2]

At the end of World War II, the country faced other economic challenges. The American economy had to be rebuilt, the returning veterans had to be incorporated back into the work force, and economic depression avoided. All the savings accumulated by defense workers during the war had to be put to some use. A major tool for the solution of these problems was believed to be the housing industry, which was encouraged to build houses in suburbia.

With an automobile in every garage ready to transport its owners beyond the city and returning servicemen eager to buy new homes, home building in the suburbs began in earnest. The federal government, through the Veterans Administration, made funds available to help veterans buy new houses or old houses in good condition. Other federal programs supported home ownership as well. Because much of the existing housing in the cities was in a dilapidated condition, the government launched a program of slum clearance (later given the more socially acceptable title of urban renewal), that would tear down the most deteriorated structures in the inner cities.

By the early 1950s the rate of middle-class suburbanization had increased. But in the cities, where more of the poor lived, the rebuilding of the urban renewal programs could not keep pace with the clearance programs. More houses were being torn down than were being built. This resulted in a net loss of housing for low-income households. As the middle and working class families moved to the suburbs, the inner-city houses they had occupied were taken over by people seeking inexpensive housing. Single young people, people on pensions, transients, and low-income families moved into the rental units in the neighborhoods surrounding the commercial cores of cities.

In St. Paul, the residential area south of Grand Avenue known both as Crocus Hill and Summit Hill had been fully built up since the mid 1930s. Julian Baird, the president of the First National Bank of St. Paul and under-secretary of the Treasury during the Eisenhower administration, was the one who started the migration out. Unable to find a suitable home or building lot in Crocus Hill, in 1938 he built a home in the elite suburb of Sunfish Lake. As soon as the construction industry gained momentum after the war, the children of many of the old families followed, moving to North Oaks, Sunfish Lake, Mendota Heights, or Dellwood, suburban locations away from the uncertainties of life in the city. This was the region's first migration, the movement of middle and upper-class households—mainly white Anglo-Saxon Protestants—out of the city into the suburbs.

Two additional migrations north of Grand occurred during the post-war period that had a significant effect on the development of the avenue. They were the departure of the Jewish population from the Hill district and the movement of the African-American population after Interstate Freeway 94 was built through the heart of their community along Rondo Street.

Members of the Jewish faith had been residents of St. Paul since the first years of the city. Large numbers of German Jews came to the Midwest in the middle of the nineteenth century. They were joined in the 1880s by refugees fleeing the pogroms of the Czar. The first Jewish settlers were not especially concentrated and lived in the middle-class neighborhoods around the State Capitol. The refugee population from Russia, however, was destitute when it arrived and was crowded into low-quality housing on the river flats across from downtown St. Paul.

As individuals in the group prospered, they moved to the area along Selby Avenue and into the residential neighborhood between Selby and Grand. Jewish merchants operated many stores and a variety of commercial establishments on Selby and were also present on Grand. As the people continued to prosper in the post-war years they moved out of the Grand Avenue area into Highland Park to the southwest. Symbolic of this movement and of the maturity of the community is the location of the synagogues. Mount Zion, the second synagogue in the United States to be built in the modern style, is on Summit Avenue. The Temple of Aaron, also in the modern style, occupies a superb location on the Mississippi River Boulevard.

When the Jewish population moved to Highland, African-Americans moved into the lower cost apartments and houses the Jewish people had occupied. The African-American population grew slowly until the 1950s since the city's few factories offered limited opportunities. Nevertheless, the community grew steadily and became concentrated along Rondo Street west of the Capitol. All this was to change when the federal highway planners and the Minnesota Department of Transportation decided to clear space through the center of St. Paul and the Rondo neighborhood for the right of way of Interstate 94.

Notes

1. Alan A. Altschuler, *The City Planning Process* (Ithaca, Cornell University Press, 1965), p. 21.

2. Gordon Schendel, "How Mobsters Grabbed a City's Transit Line," *Collier's Weekly*, September 29, 1951.

The Rondo neighborhood, looking south on Arundel from Rondo before I-94 was built. The second floor of the building on the right housed Local 516 of the International Brotherhood of Waiters and Sleeping Car Porters. (Photo courtesy of the Minnesota Historical Society.)

6

The I-94 Ditch and Its Urban Victims

THE THIRD MIGRATION in the Grand Avenue neighborhood was caused, not by increasing affluence, as were the first two, but by policies of the federal government. Soon after becomming president, Dwight Eisenhower followed through with a plan developed by Harry S. Truman for an interstate highway system to connect the entire country with limited access, multi-lane roadways. The Federal Aid Highway Act of 1956 provided for the construction of a 40,000-mile national system of freeways. Ninety percent of the cost would be borne by the federal government and ten percent by the states. Translated into dollars, that meant $400 million would be spent in the Twin Cities area and over $100 million in St. Paul alone. Local officials had the choice of taking the money for a freeway or getting nothing. If they agreed to take the freeway, they were given the task of determining the route the interstate would take.

In Minnesota, the interstate highway planning was done by engineers employed by the Highway Department, whose sole goal was the solution of traffic problems. They were frank to say they did not concern themselves with any other values or with the social problems that might come along with the throughway. It was not their job, they insisted, to consider such basic questions as to whether the presence of a throughway would be of benefit to the city or whether automobiles should be allowed to dominate cities.

The Federal Bureau of Public Roads had decreed that

the right of way of the freeway in cities should be 400 feet wide. In St. Paul, the existing right of ways were far narrower, generally only sixty feet wide. Only one street in the entire city had a right of way as wide as 200 feet. The highway department engineers laid out a proposed route for the throughway that cut a 400-foot-wide swath along the route of St. Anthony Avenue, a street parallel to and ten blocks north of Grand Avenue. Five-sixths of St. Paul's Black community lived in an area two miles long and one-half mile wide, and St. Anthony Avenue ran precisely through the center of it. The neighborhood was known as Rondo, after one of the streets, and it was a locale of small businesses, churches, and single- and two-family houses for working people.[1]

Two neighborhood groups and one lone city planner were the principal opponents of the St. Anthony route for the throughway. The city planner was George Harrold, a man of eighty-three who headed St. Paul's Planning Bureau. The entire bureau at the time consisted of three people: Harrold, his young assistant who was a recently graduated planner, and a secretary. The two neighborhoods involved in the interstate right of way were the Black community of Rondo and Prospect Park in Minneapolis, the only family neighborhood within walking distance of the University of Minnesota. The proposed freeway route, if constructed as planned through Prospect Park in Minneapolis, would take out several hundred fine middle class homes, many of them occupied by faculty.

Arrayed against these three groups was the Highway Department with its staff of engineers and its large budget for studies and data collection. Armed with the sincere belief that highway design and routing should be left to the engineering professionals and that public information and discussion should be kept to a minimum, the Highway Department carefully cultivated an image of rocklike strength tempered with amiability that slowly sapped the will of its opponents.

The most articulate of the highway opponents was the elderly city planner, Harrold, who, by 1945, had been chief planning engineer of St. Paul for twenty-five years. Harrold had an insider's understanding of the nebulous basis of the Highway Department's extensive research and traffic studies. Harrold believed that the studies were essentially worthless and argued instead that an understanding of how cities worked, long experience in metropolitan areas and a disciplined mind would enable officials to make wise judgments. Basically, Harrold was opposed to freeways in cities and deplored the "moving of thousands of people, who must give up their homes, churches, schools, neighbors and valued social contacts, who lose the institutions they have built for their pleasure and profit."

In the place of the freeway, Harrold favored and proposed a 200-foot wide right-of-way parkway on St. Anthony Avenue, half the width prescribed for the interstate system, that would be lined and divided by grass and majestic trees. Though he agreed that a freeway would carry more vehicles more quickly, he argued that it was foolish to concentrate traffic so heavily on one artery, that the highway would be a gigantic, unshaded, unsightly, noisy ditch filled with concentrated exhaust fumes.

When it became obvious that a freeway was coming through St. Paul regardless of the arguments of the opposition, Harrold developed an alternative to the St. Anthony route. Harrold's suggested route ranged about a mile north of St. Anthony and ran adjacent to the railroad tracks most of the way between downtown St. Paul and the border with Minneapolis. He had observed that the railroads and the city's main thoroughfares divided the city into "islands" often too small to permit the establishment of cohesive neighborhoods. A freeway down St. Anthony would only increase the number of these islands. If freeways were to come into the city, he reasoned, they should follow the routes of the already established railways where the dislocation of people and business would be minimal.

One of the major benefits of Harrold's plan was that it would preserve the Rondo/St.Anthony and Prospect Park neighborhoods. Harrold's plan was vigorously opposed by the highway engineers who maintained that they were traffic planners, not social engineers. Also influencing their decision was their belief that freeways could be used as a tool to remove obsolete neighborhoods, such as Rondo, at the core of cities and increase accessibility at the edge, thus encouraging commuters to move beyond the older built-up neighborhoods. The destruction of older neighborhoods, an outcome which Harrold considered disastrous to a city, the highway planners saw as a benefit.

The Black community's efforts to modify the impact of the freeway through its neighborhood met with no more success than had Harrold's work. Instead, the experience was a tragic story of governmental indifference to the needs of a victimized community. The consequences of decisions made over the highway extended far beyond that 400-foot-wide strip of land. They were later to become a factor in the decline of businesses on Selby Avenue, the stagnation of Grand, and the deterioration of St. Paul's historic hill neighborhood.

The displacement of people was not only a physical uprooting, it was a psychological blow as well—with residents uprooted emotionally from a community that had provided support and meaning to their lives. The repercussions of governmental acts in locating the highway where it did are still reverberating in St. Paul half a century later.

Two men led the opposition to the freeway in the Black community, the Rev. Floyd Massey, Jr., of the Pilgrim Baptist Church, and Timothy Howard, a barber who was president of the Rondo-St. Anthony Improvement Association, a group organized to express the views of threatened property owners. At the time of the throughway dispute, the Black community had already coped with the loss of hundreds of homes to federally funded urban renewal projects. People forced out of their sub-standard homes had been unable to find new places to live outside of the neighborhood and so had stayed in Rondo, adding to the overcrowding of the district.

Massey and Howard soon realized they had two issues with which to contend. One was opposition to the St. Anthony route of the freeway that would cut their community in half and force more than one fifth of its residents out of their homes. The second question was more subtle. If the freeway destroyed much of the Black community and those Black residents were unable to find housing elsewhere, it would create additional pressure for an open occupancy ordinance (a law making discrimination in the sale and rental of housing illegal) for which the Black community had long campaigned.

Massey and Howard decided to work on both fronts simultaneously as well as get help for those forced out of their homes. But privately, they felt they had a better opportunity to succeed with the open housing ordinance and relocation assistance than they did with changing the planned route of the freeway. They had visited the Highway Department and come away overwhelmed by the mass of data and statistics they were shown supporting the St. Anthony route.

During the early months of 1956, the major Black organizations campaigned vigorously for an open-occupancy ordinance and a city council appropriation for relocation services for those displaced by the freeway. The city council offered no support of open occupancy, and Mayor Joseph Edward Dillon refused to ask the city council for relocation

The Rev. Floyd Massey speaking at the ground-breaking for Maxfield School. (Photo courtesy of the Minnesota Historical Society.)

funds. The mayor did appoint a committee to consider what might be done to help the displaced people. However the committee never met, because, as Mayor Dillon explained, he was unable to find a chairman. The Planning Board listened to Massey's and Howard's pleas and expressed concern for the victims but then adjourned for the summer.

Frustrated by the city, Massey and Howard took their concerns to Governor Orville Freeman. Freeman referred the problem to the Commission on Human Rights, an organization with no legal power and no budget. Finally, toward the end of 1956, a subcommittee of the Commission on Human Rights decided that it would be a good idea to take a census to find out how many St. Paul families would be displaced by the freeway program in the next two years. The St. Paul Housing Authority was willing to make the survey, but it had no money available.

The Federal Bureau of Public Roads had established a policy of contributing ninety percent of the cost of relocation programs to the community if the state would contribute ten percent. This source of funds was cut off when Highway Department authorities insisted that no state agency had the authority to contribute funds for relocation programs. Moneys for this use, they maintained, would have to be directly authorized by the legislature. And the next session of the legislature was not scheduled until 1959, after most of the Black families would already have been displaced.

Eventually the Housing Authority agreed to finance the census itself and found that right-of-way acquisition and other public actions during 1958 and 1959 would displace 2,319 St. Paul families. The majority of these were poor, earning less than $3,500 a year. The Housing Authority offered to provide relocation assistance through 1959 for families displaced by the freeway if the city or the Highway Department would pay it $30,000 to cover the expenses of administering the program. No money was found. Of the Black families displaced by the freeway, the great majority found it impossible to buy or rent outside the boundaries of the Black community. The city government had failed to provide assistance to those displaced and had ignored the Black community's pleas for an open occupancy ordinance so that they would be able to move into other parts of the city.

In 1959, the St. Paul city attorney wrote an opinion contending that the state constitution precluded local action on open occupancy. Black leaders had urged the city council to pass an ordinance and let the courts decide the question of its constitutionality. The city council refused to even discuss the issue.[2]

In their negotiations with the city, the Black leadership had asked for four considerations. They wanted a fair market price for the condemned property, a fair housing law so that those who wished could move out of the immediate area, the freeway depressed to minimize the impact of the road on the neighborhood, and, finally, they wanted to stay in their homes as long as possible. The city refused the request for an open housing law. The other requests were met, albeit reluctantly.

When the government began to buy up the Rondo houses, it paid the owners market value for the property but not replacement value. Census tract number thirty-six was most affected. While the Black population was growing by fifty percent between 1950 and 1960, census tract thirty-six lost 46.7 percent of its residents, a total of 3,167 people.

Between 1950 and 1957, the entire area lost 1,477 families because of freeway construction. A total of 750 houses were razed for the I-94 right of way, and others were abandoned by their owners. By 1959, 500 houses stood vacant in the area north of Summit, and most of those occupied were in a deteriorating condition.

The construction of Interstate 94 had the effect of squeezing St. Paul's already crowded minority population into the area between the new highway on the north and Summit Avenue on the south. Highway planners predicted that the interstate would reach its peak carrying capacity sometime in the 1970s and foresaw the possible widening of Selby and Marshall Avenues to carry the projected overflow of east-west traffic. The fact that these streets were lined with substantial houses that would have to be removed if the streets were widened was considered of little importance. As a result, though the streets were never widened or any houses destroyed, the possibility that this might happen served to discourage potential investors.

Notes

1. Altschuler, pp. 22-23.
2. Altschuler, p. 64.

The ghost of an old auto parts warehouse is still visible as the building is being remodeled for a new tenant at 917 Grand Avenue. (Dave Lanegran photo.)

7

Urban Renewal: Government Efforts to Make Amends

IN THE EARLY 1950S, a large area immediately north of Grand had been designated as the Summit-University Renewal Project. This four-square-mile area—bounded by University Avenue on the north, Summit Avenue on the east and south and Lexington Parkway on the west—had been chosen through the cooperative planning of the local African-American community, the Housing and Redevelopment Authority, the city council, and the federal government.

In most respects, the Summit University Renewal Project was a reflection of the best thinking of the time. A large area was selected so the impact of the program would be maximized. A renewal plan was developed that contained plans for improving both the physical and social elements of the area. Aging sewers were to be replaced, new streets and street lighting were to be installed. This was a very ambitious project for St. Paul—nothing of this scope had ever been previously attempted.

The Summit University Renewal Area was both large and diverse. Ten thousand housing units were occupied by twenty-four thousand people. The population within the area were some of the poorest and wealthiest people of the city. The oldest families of the city lived here as well as some of the most recent arrivals. The large, well-maintained houses on Summit and the southern fringe were balanced by some of the city's worst multiple family housing toward the center and north.

The young African-American population was suffering from high unemployment. Crime rates were high, and one of the areas main intersections, Selby and Dale, known as "Hell's Kitchen," was the center of the city's drug and prostitution businesses. The Selby Avenue commercial street was deteriorating as the wealth of its trade area continued to decline.

Between 1967 and 1975, about thirty-four million dollars were spent on the area. Some twelve hundred new apartment units were built, hundreds of houses were torn down, and a like number rehabilitated. A new school was constructed, and the Martin Luther King Jr. Community Center and playground were built. The social programs of the Model Cities effort provided basic services for low-income households.

The result of this intensive effort stabilized the decline of the area, but that was about all. The basic problems persisted. There were not enough jobs. Investors were attracted to growing communities in the suburbs, and they thought Summit-University was too risky a place for investment. Large areas of land had been cleared of dilapidated structures, but new uses could not be found for the lots, so they stood empty, covered with weeds and debris. The African-American community did not have enough wealth to finance development schemes themselves, and government funds were not available. In the eyes of the more militant members of the Black community, the urban renewal efforts had failed. That failure became apparent to all when serious rioting broke out on Selby Avenue.

Selby is an older street than Grand. In 1847, Jeremiah W. Selby had purchased forty acres of land on St. Anthony Hill to raise potatoes and other vegetables. His land extended from Dayton Avenue to Summit Avenue and from the Cathedral to Dale Street. Henry Rice, a prominent early resident, thought Selby a fool to have bought land so far out of town and inaccessible because of the bluff and swamp at the eastern end of Summit. Despite these problems, the growing town expanded westward, and, by 1854, Selby Avenue had been platted and named. The first cable cars had moved up the bluff to Selby through the Selby tunnel, and commercial development took place where the trolley lines crossed at Western and Dale.

Though Selby Avenue, like Grand, had been in a slow decline for a decade, the end of the effective business community came with the 1960's politicization of the Black community. As more and more Black residents crowded onto the streets adjoining Selby Avenue, the white businesses there came to be perceived by the militant as the enemy. The attitude that certain streets of the city were to be reserved for the use of a single racial or social group provided a climate for crime and vandalism to take place.

Beginning in the early 1960s, criminal elements engaged in assaults, purse snatchings, shoplifting, muggings and destruction of property. Shootings became more frequent. As the 1960s progressed, fewer and fewer customers braved the threat of violence to walk Selby Avenue and patronize the merchants on the street. The corner of Dale Street and Selby Avenue, historically one of the busy and prosperous intersections of the city, became a watchword of urban decay and violence. The parking lot of the Cathedral became the nightly staging area for St. Paul police cars as they tried to control the violence on Selby. Monsignor Ambrose Hayden watched the fires on the street from his rooms at the Chancery.

On January 13, 1969, Black youth with baseball bats and shouting "Black Power" smashed the windows of the Delmont Barber Shop at 671 Selby, Fannie's Delicatessan at 689 Selby, Sid's Hardware at 693 Selby and Levine's Printers at 695 Selby. Many of the businesses were owned by Jewish merchants, remnants from the years when the intersection at Selby and Dale had been the center of the Jewish community. Though the police responded to the complaints about vandalism, their efforts were not vigorous or determined enough to protect the merchants on Selby Avenue. The businesses closed. After their windows also were smashed, the Lil General Store at Dale and Selby and the Sunrise Food Market also shut their doors for the last time.

The *Pioneer Press* sent a reporter to interview business owners on Selby Avenue in an attempt to discover the extent of the vandalism problem. The reporter found that twenty-three additional businesses, besides those attacked on January 13, were experiencing harassment and looting.[2] Though it expressed concern, the city did not take any major actions to protect the Jewish businesses. When store owners realized that they were to be left essentially on their own and that they could no longer get insurance for their establishments on Selby Avenue, they quietly closed their doors and moved. No other businesses, Black or White, replaced them. What had been a thriving business street for almost a hundred years was almost destroyed in a matter of months.

The Selby riots made it plain to all that the redevelopment concepts were not working and planners badly needed another idea. Surprisingly, they got it. It was called historic preservation. Although the area north of Grand had lost a large number of older buildings, it still contained the largest concentration of older residential structures in Minnesota. If these buildings could be defined as a resource or an opportunity, rather than a liability or a problem, the area could have quite a different future.

At the midpoint of the twentieth century, certain theories of urban development became popular, based, in part, on observations of how plant groups occupied space and related to each other in the competition for light and nutrients. Sociologists believed that the engine driving city growth was the expansion of the central business district. Land-use patterns in the city, they believed, were based principally on wealth and social class. According to this theory, the rich lived on the fringe of the city, the poorest in the center and the middle and working classes occupied the space in between.

This is where the concepts from plant ecology came in. The planners noticed how groups of plants moved in and took over each other's space, a process called "invasion and succession." According to these ideas, there was a correct community of people for each location—just as there was an ideal growing site for each plant type. If conditions changed, the communities—whether of plants or people—would shift. One type would invade the next and succeed it. Then the next type would invade and struggle to dominate until it succeeded the first invader. There was even thought to be some kind of natural law, akin to Adam Smith's "invisible hand," which postulated that people, like plants, would shift around, invading and retreating, until all had reached the optimum location where they could thrive the best.

Apartment houses built in the 1960s on the west end of Grand Avenue. (Dave Lanegran photo.)

In their model, the proponents of this idea, Robert Park and Ernest Burgess, had the central business district expanding into the zone of transition (which housed the poor), that surrounded it. Reacting to the pressure, the zone of transition would expand into the zone of workingmen's homes. The workers would move into the surrounding middle class areas, and the middle class would flee the working class by moving out into the higher income areas. The wealthy, seeing themselves invaded by the middle class, would move still further out. In so doing, the city would expand. The process was thought to be irreversible.[3]

This concept neatly took care of housing problems. As the populations moved outward, like crab grass taking over a lawn, the upper class would pass their housing down to the middle class, who would sell theirs to the working class. The working class would sell to the poor, all the way down the line. According to this idea, the housing market would continually provide new housing for all levels in the society and the worst housing at the center would be torn down to make way for the further expansion of the business center at the city's core.

This plant model of cities began to wilt as people observed that the population of the wealthy was not growing as fast as that of the poor. Therefore, the poor were always experiencing a housing shortage. They were over-crowded, and housing stayed in use until it decayed and collapsed. Even worse, the central business district was not always expanding—or, if it was, it was expanding toward the high-income neighborhoods and not always toward the poor ones, as it was projected to do.

With the rapid growth of the post-war suburbs, another version of the model was developed that called for the end of the dominance by the central business center and the rise of other business centers on the fringes of the city. This new concept was simplified into the doughnut model with the city center the hole in the doughnut. This model frightened city investors and raised many questions. If there were numerous city centers, where would the economic base for the downtown stores come from? What would save the eroding commercial tax base? Highway construction had wiped out much of the housing for the poor near the city center. Where could they find a place to live that they could afford?

Enter the concept of historic preservation. Early American preservationists had been patriots concerned with saving landmarks associated with national heroes. After the successful restoration of colonial Williamsburg, the concept of historic preservation received general acceptance and began to penetrate the mass culture. By the late 1970s, it was much deeper than an infatuation with nationalism or a fascination with the quaint aura of a bygone age. The new dimension of historic preservation stressed the human scale, craftsmanship, beauty, and tranquillity of older buildings and neighborhoods. It advocated a return to quality in both material culture and personal relationships. It stressed personal knowledge of neighbors and roots in communities. Its focus on the local and a sense of place was a counter trend to the modernism of the era.

The neighborhood preservation movement had three roots, all based on events of the recent past. These roots were (1) the concept of preserving buildings and neighborhoods because of their intrinsic material and historical value, (2) the fact that slum clearance had failed and community planning was taking its place, and (3) economic inflation drastically increased the price of new homes in the suburbs.

Historic preservation was considered with renewed hope because the failure of urban renewal had been so abject. The realization of the failure was wide spread, and, in the early 1970s, federal renewal programs shifted from categorical grants (in which recipients had to spend the money the way the government wanted them to) to community development block grants where people could decide for themselves how to spend the money. Block grants called for a greater democracy and increased citizen participation at all levels. The citizen participation was fast in coming, and with it came strident voices for change.

Murray Bockin and Robert Goodman, one a sociologist and the other an architect, became national spokesmen for what they believed to be a new way to plan cities. They criticized architects and city planners for being agents of central authority, accusing them of "oppression like the military and police." They believed that the plans developed by the professional planners were doomed to fail because the profession had lost contact with the people. For radical groups, represented by Bockin and Goodman, the only solution to the problems of the American inner city was to create a new culture wherein poor people would not be dependent upon urban experts but would be responsible for their own fate.[4]

This extreme view was not institutionalized, but it had an impact on many large-scale urban-renewal programs across the country. Locally it delayed and then ended the renewal programs of Cedar Riverside Associates in Minneapolis.

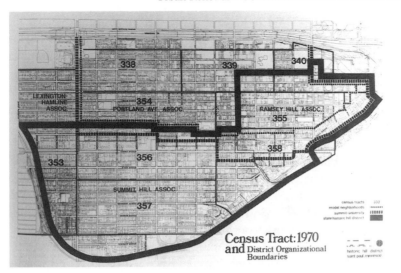

Map of the Historic Hill District, showing the locations of Summit Hill and Ramsey Hill neighborhoods. Grand Avenue is the street just below the number 353. (Laura Church photo.)

Something called district planning emerged as a compromise between the obstructionist radicals and the hierarchical structure people. Thought to be a good compromise, it pleased neither the radicals nor the old bureaucrats. The radicals opposed it because the people were still required to listen to the experts, even though the people had a part in the process. Advocates of the old style bemoaned the inefficiency of the new processes with their requirements for citizen participation and the weakening of traditional lines of communication and influence. Local politicians complained that it created a new layer of government.

District planning (also called Community Development planning) came to St. Paul in 1966 and 1967. The process was fueled by two events: the Selby riots, which brought home to everyone the failure of the urban renewal programs and the rise of a new group of urban professionals, known as community organizers.

These organizers took to the streets in the 1960s and early 1970s, urging local residents to fight freeways, hospital expansion, high rise apartment developments, and commercial expansion. In most cases, their efforts produced an interesting coalition of young radicals and middle-aged conservatives. They enjoyed enough success to give themselves confidence. At the core of the community organization movement was the notion that big government, big labor, and big business did not know how to create a livable city. All they could do was build buildings. They could not create communities. It was the folks in the neighborhood who knew how to build cities and they were against the downtown.

For a time it looked as if the "new localism" would be fueled by the enthusiasm and energy of the "new left." But fundamental economic differences between the radicals and the conservative residents of inner city areas frustrated the emerging coalition. The organizers who took up the cause of the neighborhoods after the anti-war effort of the Vietnam years soon turned to other causes or went on to careers in business and universities.

Finally, dollars and cents, the third root of the historic preservation movement, entered into the picture. The increased cost of construction and financing put new houses in the suburbs beyond the economic reach of many families of the baby-boom generation. The older upper-class neighborhoods around Grand Avenue were underpriced. The space, quality of material, and decorative details could not be duplicated in new suburbs. The older houses were seen as non-renewable resources. They would increase in value if they and their environment were maintained.

Notes

1. *Building the Future from Our Past* (St. Paul, Minnesota, Old Town Restoration, 1975), p. 14.

2. *St. Paul Pioneer Press*, January 13, 1969.

3. Ernest Burgess, "The Growth of the City," *The City*, ed. R. Park, E. Burgess, and R. MacKenzie, 1925, pp. 47-62.

4. Robert Goodman, *After the Planners* (New York: Simon & Schuster, 1971) p. 12.

Ramsey Hill house tour, 1985. (*Highland Villager* photo.)

8

Historic Preservation to the Rescue

IN THE EARLY 1970S, the area of the eastern section of Grand Avenue and the Historic Hill District was a complex set of positive and negative features. It had once been the city's premier neighborhood, but it had lost its appeal to the very wealthy. While it contained a wonderful collection of older homes with great charm, many were in a sorry state of repair. Social conditions were not good. The area was home to many troubled people, some living in group homes or halfway houses in low-quality housing. The crime rate was high. Public schools held little attraction for middle class households.

Depending upon one's point of view, the area was either blessed or cursed because ninety-four percent of the houses in Summit Hill were built before 1939. In Ramsey Hill, the clearance and rebuilding programs had reduced that percentage to eighty-four percent though, since it was larger than Summit Hill, it actually had more older buildings. Many of the houses dated from the building boom in the late nineteenth century. In Ramsey Hill only thirteen percent of the homes were owner occupied and another ten percent were vacant. This contrasted to the city wide figures of fifty-five percent owner occupied and forty-two percent rental.

Though it was not their original intent, and mostly by inadvertence, the Catholic Church in St. Paul played a major role in the preservation of a significant number of the old mansions on Summit Ave. The church's presence on Summit Avenue began as a result of two circumstances. One was

Joseph home at 365 Summit Avenue. This is the house used by the Catholic diocese to house forty-five Franciscan nuns. (Dave Lanegran photo.)

the building, in 1915, of the cathedral on the site of the Norman Kittson house across the street from the mansion of railroad builder James J. Hill. The second factor was the close friendship that developed between Hill and Archbishop John Ireland. Upon Mrs. Hill's death, the Hill mansion was willed to the Church. The estate, which was settled in 1925, stipulated that the building must be used for works of charity and education for fifty years.[1]

The church complied with Hill's request by putting the Diocesan Teacher's College in his mansion. At that time, nuns of the diocese were not allowed to attend public colleges, even such Catholic schools as St. Catherine's and St. Thomas. Instead the instructors from these schools came to the Diocesan Teacher's College in the Hill mansion to conduct classes for the nuns. Once they had graduated, many of the sisters stayed on in St. Paul, teaching at the cathedral school, which had been established in 1914 for children in grades one through eight. The decision to put a teacher's college in Hill's mansion had far-reaching consequences for Summit Avenue because the nuns, who came from all over the state to attend the college, needed housing in the vicinity of the cathedral. They found that housing in the aging mansions on Summit Avenue.

The Benedictine Sisters of Crookston, Minnesota, bought the house at 239 Summit for about thirty young sisters attending the Diocesan Teacher's College. The Rugg house at 251 Summit was purchased to house religious edu-

The Rugg house at 251 Summit Avenue. This building was used by the Church to house religious education teachers. (Laura Church photo.)

cation teachers and religious education programs. The Franciscan Sisters of Little Falls bought the mansion at 365 Summit in 1950 when the original owners failed to find any other buyers for the property. Forty-five Franciscan nuns lived there until 1966, when the house was sold to Earl Joseph. The house at 323 Summit was purchased as a home for working girls and was later used as offices for a charity bureau for rural Catholic counties.

The Alexander Wilder house, a landmark on Summit Avenue, was purchased by the Catholic Church in 1918 to be a home for Archbishop Ireland, who lived there for the last months of his life. Archbishop Dowling moved in next and lived in the house from 1919 until 1930. He was followed by Archbishop Murray who occupied the house from 1932 until 1934. Murray was a man of simple tastes and did not enjoy living in the big rambling house. When he learned that the Sisters of Notre Dame from Mankato were looking for housing for sisters attending the Diocesan Teacher's College, he moved into two rooms on the third floor of the cathedral rectory and invited the sisters to live in the house. When the Diocesan Teacher's College closed in 1950 after thirty-three years in operation, the sisters moved out of the Wilder house,

The A. H. Wilder residence at 226 Summit. The building was demolished in July 1959, and the offices of the Catholic Archdiocese were built on the site. (Photo courtesy of the Minnesota Historical Society.)

and the building was used for church offices. In 1961, the Wilder mansion was demolished to build new church offices and a residence for clergy and the archbishop.

The Boeckmann House, built by Hill's daughter and her husband at 366 Summit Avenue, was also given to the church. Archbishop Binz lived there from 1967 until 1975. When Binz moved to Chicago, the mansion was sold to John Rupp, a local developer. According to Monsignor Hayden, the property was never taken off the tax rolls of the city.

The Catholic church was a good landlord of the buildings it owned. The houses were well maintained, and the extraordinary architectural elements and craftsmanship of the Hill House, in particular, were preserved. With the exception of the Wilder house, the buildings were saved from demolition. Thanks in large part to the need for housing for nuns attending classes and teaching at the Catholic schools, the neighborhood around the cathedral and the eastern end of Summit Avenue was preserved.

Neighborhood conservation began quietly south of Summit Avenue. Encouraged by the members of old families that had remained in the houses on Summit and in Crocus Hill, younger middle-class couples began to buy up homes in the area as early as the 1950s. Among the old families who stayed in the neighborhood were the Bakers, Stringers, Wrights, Wilsons, O'Briens, Towles, Weyerhaeusers, Platts, DeCosters, Deans, Strykers, Davidsons, Cardozos, Dono-hues, McGowans, Donnellys, Jacksons, Lightners, Mind-rums, Richards, Blodgetts, Mulallys, Godfreys, and Gehans. Their names read like a who's who of the business and pro-fessional leadership of two generations of the city's history.

Though the houses in the Summit Hill neighborhood were not as grandiose as those on Summit and in Ramsey Hill, they were still large and well designed. They were also not as old nor had they been damaged as much by conver-sions during the years of housing shortages. These houses suited the large and growing families of the 1950s and 1960s. At one point, sixty-three children lived on Goodrich Avenue between Dale and St. Albans streets. There was a good ele-mentary school (Linwood) nearby and three excellent pri-vate schools in the area.

The houses themselves were bargains that appreciat-ed rapidly. Bigger and better built than the typical suburban tract home, they were also conveniently located to the gov-ernmental, financial and legal centers of employment in the downtown. In 1970, the house at 653 Goodrich with four bedrooms, three fireplaces, and an in-ground swimming pool in the back yard sold for $26,000. Roger Swardson bought it in 1974 for $40,000 and sold it in 1986 for $158,000. The house sold again in 1990 for $278,000.[2]

While the neighborhood did not attract the wealthi-est of the business community, the new people found this neighborhood a perfect place to put down roots. This devel-opment attracted very little notice in the city as a whole and is noteworthy because the process was not one of a filtering down from one socio-economic class to another. Instead, Crocus Hill and Summit Hill were occupied by a whole new group of middle and upper class households. The residents were the bureaucrats, lawyers, bankers, school administra-tors, and business people who made the system work. They were neither captains of industry nor the nouveau riche. In 1967, the Summit Hill Association was formed to represent the neighborhood in dealing with the city planning process.

Solid as the development of Summit Hill was, the exciting historic preservation drama took place in the Ramsey Hill neighborhood. By the early 1970s an obvious shift was taking place in people's attitudes toward the area at the eastern end of Summit Avenue and on Ramsey Hill. A new generation of young professional people was moving into the area who identified with the city and urban life. They did not want to raise their families in the suburbs. When they found that good, inner-city homes could be purchased for less money than smaller, less substantial suburban houses, they began buying and renovating the older buildings.

Many of these young people were veterans of the anti-Vietnam war movement. The energy they had poured into that cause now became channeled into historic preservation and renovation of the dilapidated old houses located, principally, in the area north of Summit Avenue. Following the pattern of the Summit Hill Association, in 1972 residents organized the Ramsey Hill Association to help change the image of the neighborhood. The area had been considered a high risk location by lenders and insurance agents. The organization set out to build confidence in the area's future. One of the most effective means at their disposal was house tours.

The first Ramsey Hill house tour of fourteen houses drew three thousand people. Some visitors had never been in the neighborhood before. In 1975, the house tour drew ten thousand people, many of whom had never been in St. Paul before. The new image and available funds produced a boom in renovation. About one hundred houses were purchased for restoration in 1974 and 1975 alone. A waiting list was maintained of people looking for old houses to restore.

Thanks to the efforts of Fred Norton, the representative of the area, the Minnesota Legislature passed legislation that enabled residents to form the Summit-Hill Historic District and a commission to provide architectural protection for the area. The legislation provided for long-term, low-interest loans to persons of low and moderate income if they would buy and rehabilitate the houses, and it outlawed discrimination in the lending practices. As a result of that legislation, on June 24, 1973, the area was designated an Historic District, the largest urban preservation district in the country.

Another organization, Old Town Restorations, had been formed in the mid 1960s by local residents to purchase, rehabilitate and resell deteriorated houses on Summit and neighboring streets. Old Town's big project was development of the Fitzgerald Condominiums at 475-481 Laurel Avenue. These apartment buildings, in which the author F. Scott Fitzgerald was born, were in terrible condition. Old Town put together a financial package for their conversion to condominiums with a low-interest rehabilitation loan from the St. Paul Housing and Redeveopment Agency and bank mortgages. The number of interested buyers was so great that names were drawn from a hat to select the twelve buyers.

Visitors at 550 Summit
Avenue during the Ramsey
Hill house tour in 1993.
(*Highland Villager* photo.)

Old Town continued to rehabilitate properties and
served as the major institution in the historic planning process. In 1974, it received grants from numerous organizations
including the State Arts Council, the National Endowment
for the Arts, the Northwest Area Foundation, and the geography and architecture departments of the region's colleges
and universities.

A national movement, "Back to the Cities," organized and held several conferences to report on progress in various American cities. The name was unfortunate because it implied there was a mass migration from the suburbs to the city. Detractors pointed out that none of the historic neighborhoods undergoing rehabilitation had increased in population. The discussion of population decline or gains missed the point. Neighborhood conservation did not save people or even all of the old buildings. It saved tax base and markets.

Jim Wengler and Jim Lynden produced a slide show, "New Old Town in Town," with pictures of the houses and apartments in the Ramsey and Summit Hill neighborhoods in an attempt to dispel the negative image people had of the area. The slide show was presented to more than fifty groups in the Twin Cities area, and Wengler and Lynden were invited to present it to a "Back to the Cities" conference in New York City. The response in New York was one of incredulity. The viewers there saw the pictures of the fine old brick apartment buildings going for $10,000 and asked Wengler and Lynden, "Why are you showing these pictures and letting everyone know about these bargains? You should be buying up these buildings yourselves."[3]

Initially, the city administration of St. Paul approved of the historic preservation movement. In the 1970s, the city initiated two similar programs, called BMHR (Below Market Housing Rehabilitation) and BMIR (Below Market Interest Rate), in an effort to stimulate interest to rehabilitate deteriorating buildings. The BMHR program provided $40,960,700 at nine and three-quarters percent interest to moderate income individuals if they would buy deteriorating houses in the area and fix them up. The BMIR program offered $41,945,000 at eight and one-quarter percent.

The response to both programs was tremendous. Within a three-year period, 274 condominiums and 576 single-family houses were rehabilitated mainly by young homeowners and principally in the Summit and Ramsey Hill neighborhoods. They called themselves "Urban Pioneers." The majority of the home buyers, 92.6 percent, were young white couples, 4.9 percent were Black, and the remainder were Hispanic or Asian. The average sale price of a home was $69,423, with the average loan at $61,389. Interestingly, the goal of the program was not "historic preservation," though that was a prime concern (along with affordable housing) for many of the buyers, but "to promote and facilitate the rehabilitation of deteriorated housing in Saint Paul regardless of the income of the purchasers."[4]

The loan program ended when the money ran out. Though it had been a resounding success in making home ownership available to hundreds of individuals and families otherwise unable to afford it and the program preserved and rehabilitated many blocks of houses, it was not renewed. One of the principal reasons for non-renewal was the concern that renters were being forced out of their houses—though the evaluations of the two programs found that this was not the case. Nevertheless, the African-American community and advocates for the poor objected to the loan program, claiming that the poor were being forced out of their homes and out of the area by the middle-class white professionals who were buying and fixing up the houses.

The preservationists countered that the process was a plan to save a neighborhood and that, in any case, the poor deserved better than dilapidated and deteriorating buildings in which to live. The poor had been living in the houses until the buildings literally fell down. Then they moved on. How, the preservationists asked, did that help either the poor or the city? There were other programs available to provide housing assistance for the poor.

In the end, the preservationists lost. The city gave in to the demands of those who feared gentrification, and, despite its success, the loan program was not renewed. When the program ended, public and private investment in the area slowed, and little additional rehabilitation occurred. But the gains had been substantial. Hundreds of buildings had been saved, houses and yards had been fixed up, and much of the area had clearly been reclaimed.

A researcher studying the preservation process in Ramsey Hill during the mid 1970s found that forty-three percent of the owners surveyed had lived in the area less than six years; twenty-six percent had been there less than twelve months. These urban pioneers were essentially young people; seventy-four percent were twenty-one to thirty-nine years old, were married but without children. While their income varied widely, most had finished at least four years of college and were employed in professional and managerial positions. They had moved into the area to pursue a lifestyle revolving around a house that required investments of taste, work, and resources. The houses were viewed as relatively inexpensive and distinctive. All were enthusiastic about building a new neighborhood. Though the loan program ended, the gradual fixing up of houses continued—improvements moving west at about a mile a decade. With the business community on Selby in steep decline, these new residents looked for services south across Summit Avenue to Grand.

Notes

1. Interview by Billie Young with Monsignor Ambrose Hayden, July, 1995.

2. Interview by Billie Young with Roger Swardson, August 10, 1995.

3. Telephone interview by Billie Young with Jim Wengler, July 6 and 12, 1995.

4. Jim Bellus, *BMHR* and *BMIR* (Department of Planning and Economic Development, St. Paul, Minnesota, September, 1982).

5. Sonia Mykleton, masters thesis, University of Minnesota.

6. Interview by Billie Young with John Rupp, April 5, 1995.

The oldest commercial building on Grand Avenue. This building is located between Snelling and Cambridge Avenues on the north side of Grand. The earlier picture (bottom) was taken in the 1890s, the second (top) about one hundred years later. (Photos courtesy of David Lanegran.)

9

Grand Avenue Organizes to Fight Blight

THE DESTRUCTION OF THE SELBY AVENUE business community and the deterioration of the neighborhood had a profound
effect on Grand and delayed its renaissance for at least ten
years. Grand Avenue business owners had watched with
mounting concern as slowly, block by block, the blight and
violence moved south from Selby toward Grand. They feared
that soon Grand Avenue would suffer the same fate that had
befallen Selby Avenue.

As Grand Avenue merchants saw what was happening, they, one by one, went out of business or relocated. In
l962, Ramaley's closed its food and catering business, retain-
ing only the liquor sales, and razed part of its building for a
parking lot. The Corner Grocery was held up twice by armed
robbers, and, as a result, Isadore Harry Yugend reluctantly
closed his store.

Hold-ups became a daily occurrence on Grand
Avenue, and many businesses that remained open locked
their doors during the day, unlocking them only when a customer knocked or rang a bell. Knowledgeable business and
community leaders believed that the avenue was going into
a fatal decline. They saw the market collapsing, believed the
city itself was decaying and were trying to find a way to get
out of business without losing too much of their money.
They were frightened by the crime rate in the area and especially by the presence of young Black males.

The owner of Larry's Dairy in the 1600 block of
Grand always locked his business after school hours to keep

the groups of junior-high-age boys out, and he kept a baseball bat behind the counter for enforcement and intimidation. When rumors circulated one day that there was going to be trouble on Grand Avenue, Buz Thorne sat up all night in front of the windows of his Grand Avenue Liquor store with a shotgun in his lap. "We were worried that this part of town would turn into another Selby Avenue. Men would get together to talk about where they were going to move their businesses off Grand Avenue."[1]

Some businesses reported that their insurance agents had recommended they install grates over the store windows to prevent the smash-and-snatch robberies that had taken place on Selby. While business owners were aghast at such insensitive advice, they saw their insurance rates go up after the Selby fires. Banks red-lined the area, refusing to lend money for new business development on the street. The police department advised would-be business owners not to locate on Grand because of the high crime rate.

The old buildings that lined the street were considered not an asset but a liability. When Bill Wengler bought his house on Lincoln, one block off Grand Avenue, in 1972 for $28,000, his co-workers at St. Paul Public Works laughed at him. They believed the area was doomed, only a few steps away from housing dirty book stores. Many buildings on Grand were standing empty or were under-utilized. Those who looked into the future of Grand Avenue could see nothing but blight ahead for the street.

That blight did not come to any disastrous extent was due to a remarkable combination of people and circumstances. In February 1966, a small group of business owners and a dentist organized the Grand Avenue Business Association in a defensive move to protect the street. Rather than sit passively by as their fellow business people closed their shops, these few activists decided to organize and try to slow the downward trend. Their primary concern was the growing incidence of crime on the street.

Wally Peters remembers that the idea for a Grand Avenue Business Association first occurred to him in the early 1960s when Wendell Fritz, a retired cookie salesman, came into Peter's paint and wallpaper store at 796 Grand asking for a donation for flowers for a new restaurant opening on the street. Peters thought buying flowers for newcomers could be better handled by a business association. Fritz agreed, so he and Peters called a meeting of about fifteen business owners at Port's Tea Room to talk about organizing a business association. While they all understood that a need

Port's Tea Room Building built over the Oxford Club ravine. (Dave Lanegran photo.)

existed, most were pessimistic. The street was too long for an association, they reasoned. Several attempts had already been made to organize, and all had failed.

Despite the pessimism, a core of business people continued meeting, culminating in an organizational meeting held at Tony Muska's Lighting Center. Mayor George Vavoulis attended. At this meeting the Grand Avenue Business Association formally organized with Wally Peters the first president. Though not yet legally incorporated, with no money and few members, they selected three goals for the fledgling organization: the reduction of crime on Grand, the improvement of street lighting, and repair of the surface of the street. Grand Avenue was in such disrepair that the automobile dealers joked that, "You could drive a car down Grand Avenue, and, if it came back in one piece, it was a good car."

Though an association had been organized, few gave it much of a chance for survival until George Buck, who owned the Ford dealership at Grand and Victoria, organized a dinner for the group at his golf club. Wendell Fritz went up and down Grand Avenue selling tickets to the dinner, and, to everyone's amazement, 165 business people attended the event. Among those attending were Jim Gobolish, vice president of the Grand Avenue bank and some of his board members. They must have been impressed by the enthusiasm and the attendance because the next morning Gobolish appeared at Wally Peter's paint store with a check for $1,000 for the Grand Avenue Business Association. The money had been left on deposit from former abortive efforts to set up a business association. "You are on your way," said Gobolish when he gave the check to an astonished Peters.

Peters used the money to hire attorney Bob Gearin to incorporate the association. The incorporators, who also served as the first board of directors, all with one year terms, were Peters, Irving Lebo, who owned a drug store at Grand and Hamline, Louise Bailey, who sold sheet music and records from her red brick home at 727 Grand Ave (the oldest remaining residence on the street)[2]; Dr. William Chopp, a dentist at 611 Grand; Dorothy R. Fahey, at 908 Grand; Lucille Barnes, who ran an interior decorating business out of her three-plex home at 1011 Grand, John Karayusuf, at 1571 Grand, Al Grove, who had a car dealership at 1330 Grand, Martin Olson, a baker who owned the Bungalow Bakery at 1080 Grand, Audrey Winger, who had a women's clothing store at 1662 Grand, and Donald Smolik, who owned the Grand Avenue Ace hardware store at 1676 Grand.

The avenue this group set out to protect and preserve was still a street of small craftsmen, though the number of small shops was far less than it had been in 1930. The *City Directory* of 1930 listed more than 250 businesses on the entire length of the street, reflecting the fact that the Grand Avenue community of that time was self-sufficient. An extensive network of small businesses supplied the goods and services within walking distance of most of the residents of the street.

By 1970, much of that had changed. Only one shoe repair shop, Henry's at 672½ Grand, served the Avenue where, in 1930, five "shoe rebuilders" were kept busy. From having a drug store on almost every corner between Dale and Lexington, the number had dropped to three. The number of grocery stores had also declined from thirty-nine to four, and there were no longer tinners, upholsterers, caterers, dressmakers, stencilers, carpenters or tailors at work on the street. Gone was the Radio Girl Perfume Company.

In place of these lost businesses were a stained-glass studio, a furniture refinisher, picture framers, a gift shop, dry cleaning establishments, automobile showrooms, five restaurants, auto body shops, gas stations and several businesses wholesaling auto parts and electrical supplies. The streetcar tracks and brick paving had been buried. The cream-colored carved stonework of the Studebaker building at Grand and Victoria was covered with sheets of blue aluminum siding. Grand Avenue in 1970 was a tired, neglected urban strip—ugly, unloved and about to be abandoned to a fate of decay and disintegration.

One of the reasons this did not happen was the energy and determination of the small group of business owners including the dentist, Dr. William Chopp. Doc Chopp, as he was called, had moved onto the avenue in 1946 when he returned from service in World War II. He bought the house at 607 for his residence and opened his dental practice at 611 Grand. When the street began to deteriorate in the 1960s, Chopp realized that the success of his dental practice was tied to the success of Grand Avenue as a whole. The declining reputation of the street was brought to his attention most forcibly when the mother of a dental hygienist he wanted to hire for his office refused to allow her daughter to work for him because of her fear of armed violence on Grand. At that point Doc Chopp took it upon himself to change the street.[3]

Dr. William Chopp, known affectionately as "Doc Chopp" took Grand Avenue's safety and beauty very seriously. (Photo courtesy of Barbara Chopp.)

As one of the organizers of the Grand Avenue Business Association, Chopp began by lobbying city hall for a foot patrolman to walk up and down Grand Ave. But Doc Chopp did not leave that policing task solely to the authorities. Chopp walked the avenue himself. Wednesday was his day off from his dental practice, and he spent that day walking Grand, visiting every business on the street with a message of encouragement and optimism. His daughter and wife remember that every night, for many years, Chopp would load his family into the car and drive the full length of Grand Avenue, "putting the street to bed" as he called it before turning in himself for the night.

One day Chopp heard about an attempt to extort protection money from a Grand Avenue business. Chopp conducted a private investigation of his own, and, when he was sure he knew who the culprit was, he put his .38 pistol in his pocket, drove to the suspect's place of business and confronted him. Though Chopp was not a large man, he was strong, and he was fearless. "He wasn't afraid of anyone or anybody," remembers his wife, Barbara. The extortionist made no more attempts on Grand Avenue.

One evening, Chopp and his family were returning from their nightly trip on the street when he observed some young women loitering at the Grand and Dale intersection. Suspicious, Chopp parked his car and walked down the street only to be solicited by the women. Though he said nothing to the young women, the next morning Chopp called on the owner of the Red Carpet Sauna, a business located next door to Chopp's dental office. After that visit, there was no more soliciting on the street by the young women from the sauna.

Chopp was the fifth president of the Grand Avenue Business Association. The monthly meetings were held in his office, where he enlivened the sessions and ensured a good attendance of the board by serving samples of his home-made wine. His wine-making began when he grew an overabundance of gooseberries on his farm. Not knowing what else to do with them, he made wine. The wine "didn't work" according to his wife, so he fermented the mixture again and turned it into champagne. That turned out to be drinkable, and, intrigued by the chemistry of the process, Chopp went on to make wine from cranberries and varieties of grapes.

Officer Dan Collins patrolling the Grand Avenue beat in response to neighborhood association pressure. (Photo by Elberta Matters.)

Doc Chopp, with others on the board of the association such as Ray Myers, Wally Peters, and Don Smolik, became the social directors of the avenue. In an attempt to create a spirit of camaraderie among the business owners, they organized quarterly membership meetings that involved dinners at exotic locations. They held mystery bus trips to places such as the Lowell Inn in Stillwater or to a game farm for dinner. One meeting was a pig roast dinner. If a bus had been chartered for the trip, they saw to it that champagne was served on the bus.

Peters credits the quarterly social events with bringing the avenue together. "They would never have come to meetings," said Peters, "but they would come to a party." Chopp's goal was to unify the business owners into a strong enough group to have influence in city hall. Chopp, himself, was often the one to carry the avenue's requests to the city. "Who says it can't be done?" was his constant challenge when problems would arise.

Once police visibility on Grand had been achieved, the association turned to the task of improving the appearance of the street. The officers of the association called Milt Rosen, Commissioner of Public Works, to a meeting of "the boys" in the basement of Pedro's Supper Club on Grand. Though the street was not scheduled for repaving or new lights until the 1980s, they made a persuasive case for immediate improvements. No minutes were kept of the meeting, but, in a few months, repair and lighting schedules were changed, and improvements began on Grand. Business owners also did their part. The association offered prizes to businesses that had the best store front or to those that had cleaned up the alley, urging business owners to paint the alley side of their buildings as well as the front.

Don Smolik was the second president of the association when they decided to put on a jazz and art festival in the football field at Macalester College. The organizers made the mistake of scheduling it on a day that was both the fishing opener and Mother's Day. Then they compounded their error by charging $1.00 admission. Though the association lost $800 on the event, they felt they gained great publicity for the avenue when the entire rotogravure section of the St. Paul paper was devoted to the festival.

Queen contests followed soon after, to take advantage of the St. Paul Winter Carnival promotions. For a twenty-five dollar entry fee, businesses could promote a young woman for Grand Avenue Queen, who would then go on to compete city-wide to become queen of the Winter Carnival.

The original electric light fixture installed at the intersection of Grand Avenue and Dale Street. The fixture was preserved by Doc Chopp and set up in the front yard of his home on Grand. (Dave Lanegran photo.)

The contests were popular, with young women's portraits featured in store windows the length of the avenue. The final selection of a queen was made at the Queen Pageant, held at the Prom Ballroom. An undated issue of the *Drummer Boy*, the newsletter of the association, reports on one such Queen Pageant, probably held in 1971.

> We had 31 lovely girls to choose from. The dinner was excellent and very well served and there was dancing after the formalities. Wally Peters [of Color Key at Grand] did his usual fine job as Master of Ceremonies. We came within $150 of breaking even on the Pageant and this includes entry fee [for] the Winter Carnival and clothes for the queen, band at the Pageant, singers during the program, flowers for tables and the winners of the contest, trophies for the three winners and the engraving of them. It also includes the ribbon for the candidates names, photographs, a buffet supper given for the candidates by Lucille Barnes. There was a large facsimile of the *Drummer Boy* on stage, made for us by Jack Vokoun of Peters Color Key, which made a fine backdrop for the girls to stand in front of.

Barnes went on to report, "It [the Pageant] was a great deal of work, but there were many interesting and pleasant memories for the members of the committee; also that we should have five judges."[4]

In the same issue, Chopp, who was the association president at the time, appealed for new members, writing,

> How would you like to have 110 people working for you to protect your Grand Avenue investment? People such as [here he lists forty business people on the street]. They have been and are willing to, work for you, free, in fact to donate their time and some pocket money. Through their efforts, Grand Avenue's name is kept before the public with queen pageants, art and jazz festivals, concerts on Macalester College mall, and advertising. Through their efforts Grand Avenue has had new paving and lights, is being maintained and they have placed a motion before the City Council to re-name Oakland Avenue to Grand Avenue.

The renaming of Oakland to Grand was probably Doc Chopp's most amazing accomplishment. When Interstate 94 was planned, the route for Interstate 35 was also laid out with an interchange projected to be at Oakland Avenue. Grand Avenue at the time went straight east from Dale Street up what is now known as Grand Hill and ended at the bluff behind the Livingston-Griggs House.

Oakland was the street that curved down from Summit Avenue, crossed Grand east of Dale and went on south to connect to West Seventh. Grand Avenue was a street with a dead end at either end, rather like a country with no outlet to the sea. Doc Chopp looked at a map and saw Oakland Avenue and Ramsey Street, down on the flats, as Grand's outlet to all the customers who would come to Grand in the future if it could only be connected to the proposed Interstate 35. But the connection could not be allowed to say "Oakland." It had to say "Grand Avenue."

Doc Chopp, Wally Peters, and Ray Myers set out to change the names of Oakland and Ramsey streets to Grand. Before it could be taken to the City Council, however, they had to get the signatures and approval of every property owner who would be affected by the change. As they trudged door to door on Oakland and Ramsey, they found that the property owners were not concerned about the change in name. What they did not want was the trouble and expense of putting up new house numbers. Chopp solved that problem by promising to put up new house numbers on every house, at his own expense. That persuaded them.

The residents on Grand Avenue up the hill and east of Oakland were not concerned about the cost of changing house numbers. They did not want to give up the name of "Grand" for their street. Barbara Chopp remembers that her husband came home worried and discouraged about the project after visiting with these Grand Avenue residents. She listened to his explanation of the problem, thought a minute and then suggested that the name, "Grand Hill," be given to that end of the street. Doc Chopp took the name to the residents, most of whom liked it, and he gained their approval.

The last step in the process was taking the suggestion to city hall and getting the city council's approval. Roger Swardson was among the Grand Avenue Business Association members who presented the petition. As he listened to the city council members debate the issue and heard the arguments of those opposed to the name change, he deduced

Wuollet Bakery named a sourdough bread after Doc Chopp and used this photo in their publicity. (Photo courtesy of Wuollet Bakery and Barbara Chopp.)

A view down the section of Grand Avenue that was formerly Oakland Avenue. This is where Doc Chopp personally put up new house numbers on the houses after he and Wally Peters convinced the residents to change the name of their street. (Dave Lanegran photo.)

that the city council was in basic agreement with the Grand Avenue merchants but that they needed a reason to vote in favor of the petition. On the spot, he conjured up the "doctrine of felt need," explaining to the city council members that the merchants "felt need" for an outlet on the proposed new throughway was greater than the residents "felt need" to keep the old name of Grand Avenue.[5]

The city council members accepted this bit of philosophy, and the request was granted. Oakland and Ramsey became Grand Avenue all the way south to West Seventh. Grand Avenue east of Oakland became Grand Hill. And Doc Chopp made good on his promise and, by himself, changed every house number on every building on what had formerly been Oakland Avenue and Ramsey Streets.

The sustained, year after year efforts of Doc Chopp, Bob Hylton, Don Bober, Norm Geiger, Wally Peters, Don Smolik, Ray Myers, Pete Willwerscheid, Jane Teigen, Jim Solin, Bob McClay, Jim Wuollet, Bill Skally and other officers of the Grand Avenue Business Association were critical to the eventual revitalization of Grand. Led by Ernie Winter, Irene DeVinney, and later, Mimi Doran, the association members by a thousand small individual acts held the avenue together so that it could become the incubator for scores of new businesses.

One of the first of the new businesses, founded in the spring of 1972 by two neighborhood women, was the Old Mexico Shop. The experience of the Old Mexico Shop was a powerful demonstration to other potential business owners that, contrary to everyone's expectations of failure, the time had come when new businesses could once again thrive on Grand Avenue.

Notes

1. Interview by Billie Young with Wally Peters, August 29, 1995.

2. The house was later moved to Summit Avenue to make room for a Pier 1 import store on the site.

3. Interview by Billie Young with Barbara Chopp, May 22, 1955.

4. *Drummer Boy*, undated issue (probably 1971) of the newsletter of the Grand Avenue Business Association in the possession of Barbara Chopp.

5. Swardson.

10

A New Store Opens and Survives

In May 1972, two neighbor women, Mary Wilson and Billie Young set out to find a place in which to open a business. Their homes were on Crocus Hill, just two blocks south of Grand Avenue. Wilson and Young were two middle-aged, middle-class housewives who had never been in business before, had never worked for a retail business and had no immediate family members who were in business. What they *had* done was go to Mexico, fill a station wagon with folk arts and crafts and hold a sale on the third floor of Young's home. The sale had been successful, so much so that, on the basis of that experience alone, they decided to open a store.

They began their search for a store location by driving up and down Grand Avenue. Businesses on the street in 1972 consisted of two hardware stores, two or three restaurants, one bank, some bars, an antique store, a gift shop, plumbing establishments, a frame shop, gas stations, automobile dealerships, and two auto body shops. There were few pedestrians. Patrons of the businesses drove their cars to the entrances, went in, transacted their business and left in their cars. There was little strolling shop to shop. Always present was a fear of crime on Grand and in the surrounding neighborhood.

The only exception to this buttoned-up attitude was at the western end of Grand, which housed Macalester College. Here the college bookstore, men's and women's clothing stores, and campus eating establishments livened up

650 Grand Avenue (top) taken in 1957. Note brick streets. The trolley tracks had been covered over. The Hamline Auto Body Shop (bottom) at the same location and the Wig City shop that became the Old Mexico Shop. 1970 photo. (Photos courtesty of Hamline Auto Body Shop.)

the neighborhood. Students were a presence on the sidewalks, jay-walking across the street, hanging out on the corners. They would have occupied tables at sidewalk cafes and coffee houses, but St. Paul did not yet allow restaurants to serve patrons food and drink (even coffee) on the sidewalks.

Dining at a table on the sidewalk was not considered proper public behavior by the city officials of St. Paul in the 1970s.

Despite the shabbiness of Grand Avenue, the two prospective business owners never considered any other location for their store. Grand Avenue was near their homes, but, beyond the factor of personal convenience, they sensed that, with all of its problems, Grand was not guilty of the sin of dullness. Though the street was not exactly lively, there was diversity, the diversity of service businesses—dry cleaners, plumbers, fast food establishments, the shoe repair shop, and the college.

They had made two circuits of Grand Avenue looking for a store to rent and were about to give up for the day when Wilson noted a hand-lettered "For Rent" sign in a window of a store front set back from the line of buildings on the street. The window was part of the Hamline Auto Body Shop, and the building was set back from the street to accommodate the driveway where damaged cars were parked awaiting repair. The location did not appear to be conducive to retail success. It was a half block west of Dale street. East of the shop was a dry cleaner and a plumber and to the west was the body shop and a bar.

The former tenant of the store space was a woman named Doris who had a wig shop. Her sole employee, a young man, had been injured in an assault by an armed robber. Doris, who had neglected to pay workman's compensation for her employee, was left with his medical bills and a strong distaste for doing business on Grand Avenue.

Despite the discouraging history of the space, Mary Wilson and Billie Young opened the Old Mexico Shop there in June 1972. No one, except the two women owners, expected the business to survive. The landlord was George Huber, the owner of the Hamline Auto Body Shop. He offered no lease nor did the women think to ask for one. On the first day of every month Wilson would walk over to the office of the auto body shop and give the secretary a check for $150—one month's rent.

The Old Mexico Shop sign that hung from the Hamline Auto Body Shop sign at 650 Grand Avenue. (Photo courtesy of Billie Young.)

There were certain disadvantages to renting store space from an auto body shop. First was the noise. The wall was thin between the Old Mexico Shop and the area where the men worked on the cars. When they were cutting or pounding on metal with their power tools, the women and their customers had to shout to be heard above the racket. It was difficult to talk on the telephone.

The second problem was the fumes. Odors of paint thinner and solvents hung in the air. At times the women became giddy from the gasses that leaked through the cracks in the wall. But, despite the problems, more significant factors favored the survival of the new business. The rent was low. The dry cleaners brought a steady foot traffic of customers dropping off and picking up their clothes, who then discovered the Old Mexico Shop next door. The surrounding neighborhood contained residents with sophisticated middle-class tastes and interests. These people were delighted to see a new business, even one as small and tenuous as the Old Mexico Shop, open on Grand, and, once they discovered it, they gave it their patronage.

By most retail standards, the store was primitive. The two owners did everything themselves, building most of their shelves and display pieces from scrap lumber in their basements. Unaware that St. Paul had a sign ordinance (or unwilling to pay the fee for a permit), they constructed their own outdoor sign and hung it from the Hamline Auto Body standard on a Sunday morning when inspectors would presumably be in church. Such improvisation was standard procedure for small businesses establishing themselves on Grand Avenue in the 1970s.

The business flourished, and, three years after opening the Old Mexico Shop, the partners purchased the house across the street from the shop at 653 Grand. A boarding house in the 1930s, it had most recently been used as a rooming house for students and was in a run-down condition. Their plan was to restore it and turn it into a space for retail shops and a restaurant. Named the Market House, it was Grand Avenue's second mini-mall. The renovation went well, and, when it was completed, chef Don James put in The Restoration, one of the first new restaurants to open in years on Grand Avenue.

One morning soon after opening, as the dining room was filling up with guests for the noon meal, James discovered that the water to the building had been turned off by the city. With new owners, there had been a mix-up in recording payments for water bills, and the city had turned off the water for a presumed non-payment of the water bill. James came racing across the street to the Old Mexico Shop for help.

While Billie got on the telephone to the city water department, Mary and Don filled pots and pans with water and ran with them across Grand Avenue to the restaurant kitchen to get the noon meal underway. For almost two hours, until city workers got the manhole in the street opened up and the water turned back on, Don, in his white

Mary Wilson and Billie Young in front of the Market House at 653 Grand Avenue. Photo taken in 1975. (Photo courtesy of the *Pioneer Press/Dispatch.*)

chef's hat and apron, and Mary dodged traffic on Grand carrying sloshing pans of water from the Old Mexico Shop to keep the restaurant in operation.

The new businesses that opened up on Grand during this period were small individual enterprises. Their existence depended on improvisation, hard work, self-confidence, and the willingness of their owners to do a variety of tasks. Many of the owners were in business for the first time and were unimpeded by ideas of what they could or could not do. Most exhibited a high degree of self-reliance. Sales in the new businesses were, for the most part, modest but so were expenses. Because of the low rents, there was room for experimentation and a certain latitude for errors and learning the rudiments of business on the job.

While the Old Mexico Shop and the Market House with the Restoration Restaurant, candy store, basement gift shop (called Under Grand), book store (Paperback Traders), and jewelry store (Desert Gems) were six new businesses on the street that signaled to the community that something was happening on Grand Avenue, they were also small, essentially fragile enterprises. It took a young MIT graduate in architecture, Jim Wengler, and his three friends to bring stability, through the development of Victoria Crossing, to the business community on the street. Jim Wengler was a remarkable case of creativity meeting opportunity.

Victoria Crossing West Mall at Grand Avenue and Victoria Street. (James Stolpestad photo.)

11

Victoria Crossing Comes to Grand

THE STORY OF VICTORIA CROSSING begins with the *Grand Gazette* and its editor, Roger Swardson. Swardson, a former police reporter for the *Cincinnati Inquirer*, had been employed by Macalester College in its office of information services. As part of the college's outreach program, Swardson attended neighborhood association meetings. He then began to work with the Grand Avenue Business Association. There he conceived the idea of a street newspaper. He began to plan a monthly paper he called the *Grand Gazette,* and, in August 1973, when he left Macalester, he published his first issue.

Taking his cue from the Victorian houses in the neighborhood, Swardson adopted a Victorian theme for the paper. Resolving to publish no photographs, Swardson instead used the steel engravings from *Harper's Weekly* and *Leslie's Illustrated,* the two leading national newspapers of the nineteenth century, which were available as copyright-free clip art. His Christmas issue featured an illustration of Union soldiers coming home from the Civil War. The *Gazette* became an instant success with readers, if not with advertisers. Within six months, Swardson had subscribers all over the country, four in Paris and two in Accra, Ghana.

Swardson had been working on his paper out of his home on Goodrich Avenue. When that became increasingly difficult, he looked around the neighborhood for an office to rent. Walking down Grand Avenue one day, he spotted a small "For Rent" sign with a phone number on the building

James Stolpestad, one of the four original investors in Victoria Crossing, in his office at Exeter Realty Corp. He emerged as one of the principal players on Grand Avenue. (Sarah Lambert photo.)

Jim Wengler, the architect of Victoria Crossing, in the dining room of the Victoria Garden restaurant in Victoria Crossing East. (*Highland Villager* photo.)

on the northwest corner of Grand and Victoria. He called the number, and an obviously elderly woman answered the phone in a faint voice. When he asked about renting an office in the building, the voice replied, "Oh, we haven't rented an office in years. I wouldn't recommend it."

Swardson persisted and asked for a meeting. The woman agreed. She brought an elderly companion with her, both of whom were relatives and trustees of the William H. Tilden Estate, former owners of Tilden Cloverleaf Produce Company. The Tilden company had constructed the building in 1923. Besides the building on the northwest corner of Grand and Victoria, the estate also owned the garage behind the building and the building on the southeast corner of Grand and Victoria. The elderly couple was genuinely reluctant to rent space to Swardson. "It's too much trouble to rent," they said. "Why don't you buy the building?" The asking price was $125,000.

Swardson was interested, but he didn't have the money. He called his friend, James Stolpestad, a young attorney who had recently moved into the neighborhood. Stolpestad immediately said, "Let's buy it." He called two other people, his law partner Steve Smith and James Wengler, and, within a week, the four had met to figure out how they could buy the building. None of them had any experience buying commercial property. Smith thought to ask what the rents were.

The tenants in the building at the time were the Crocus Hill Drug, which paid $450 a month rent, and three small shops; Jane Wilder Prest's yarn shop, Kohner and Fredric Florists, and DeWitts Beauty Shop. Each of the small shops paid $125 per month. DeWitts was popular with the elderly women of the neighborhood, who went there for "finger waves." Upstairs three of the twelve offices were rented for fifty dollars a month, one to Dr. Venton W. Knechtges, a dentist well-known for the false teeth and bridge work he constructed, another to a retired dentist who rarely came to the office, and the third to an insurance agent. The rest of the dozen offices in the building were vacant and had been for decades.

Smith told his associates that a rule of thumb for buying property was to pay ten times the net or five times the gross. Five times the gross was $67,500. They decided that would be their first offer, which the four of them presented to the trustees of the Tilden Estate, the estate's attorney, and the realtor Bill Clapp from the Clapp Thomssen Agency. To their great surprise, it was accepted.

Grand Avenue State Bank at Grand and Victoria. This picture shows the two buildings that were combined by James Wengler to create Victoria Crossing West. The photo was taken between 1926 and 1930. (Photo courtesy the Minnesota Historical Society.)

Victoria Crossing West at the northwest corner of Grand and Victoria. (Laura Church photo.)

Each partner had to come up with $1,900 dollars for his share of the down payment. None of them had much cash, and they resorted to creative methods to find the money. David Heider, the owner of a small downtown bank, solved the down payment problem for Wengler when he suggested that Jim set up checking plus at his bank and take out an unsecured advance on the account. Swardson went to Donald Dick, president of First Bank Grand, for a loan of $1,900 to pay his share. He was turned down. Dick told him that buying the building was a bad deal. Swardson then called Andrew Boss of the St. Anthony Park State Bank. Boss came down to Grand Avenue, looked over the building and lent Swardson money for the down payment.[1] The two other partners solved their financial problems in similar ways.

Once they owned the building, Wengler moved his architecture office into one of the vacant spaces on the second floor, and Swardson took another office for the *Grand Gazette.* The name for the building, Victoria Crossing, was suggested by Roger's wife, Pam Swardson. When the new owners were going through and examining their property, trying out keys and opening doors, they found a large room on the second floor filled almost to the ceiling with pornographic literature and magazines. A second room also contained a large quantity of the materials. Apparently one of the tenants had been a subscriber, and, as the magazines arrived, he had simply tossed them into one of the empty rooms.

The new owners made some changes. They got rid of the pornography (or most of it. Wengler later delighted in leaving an example on Swardson's desk for him to find when he came to his office in the morning) and they raised the rent. DeWitt's Hair Design salon had been paying $125 a month for 1,000 square feet of space including the utilities and a full basement. When the partners inspected the basement, they found that unreported electrical fires had occurred. Also, about a dozen non-functioning washers and dryers took up basement space. When one of the washers or dryers used by the hair salon for laundering and drying towels quit, DeWitt had just shoved it aside and bought another one. DeWitt had also not bothered to vent the dryers and the basement was plastered with lint. The partners raised the rent to $250 a month. DeWitt decided that was outrageous and moved out. Other tenants either left on their own or were asked to leave. Kohner and Fredric were eased out in favor of florist Craig Olson, and the three Heath women who put in a store called Heath Plus.[2]

The first issue of the *Grand Gazette,* Volume 1, Number 1, published in August 1973 carried an advertisement for office space in Victoria Crossing. A prospective tenant could rent 130 square feet for forty-five dollars a month. The amenities included a "unique glass corridor, terrazzo floor, maple woodwork, and marble hallways."

In 1974, a fire broke out in an electrical window sign of the drugstore that severely damaged that section of the building. The fire was just the opportunity the four partners needed to reevaluate their partnership. Early on in their relationship, they had discovered that, while they were friends, they did not make good business partners. All four saw the

development possibilities inherent in the intersection, but
they had different goals and varying tolerances for risk. For
example, Wengler looked at the sidewalk in front of the
building, which had been cut back to permit the parking of
cars, and proposed that it be widened so that trees could be
planted and lights installed on the boulevard. Steve Smith
saw the sidewalk widening as a needless expenditure, while
to Jim it was necesssary for the esthetics of the building.[3] The
two attorneys wanted to invest their time and energy in the
practice of law. Swardson was expanding his neighborhood
newspapers. When the fire occurred, Wengler's three partners discussed taking the insurance money and selling the
building. This idea did not appeal to Jim, the architect, who
had not yet realized his dream for the building.

When Wengler and his partners had first looked at
the intersection of Grand and Victoria, which contained
three substantial buildings and an empty lot, they had all
thought "small urban malls." They already owned one of the
buildings. On the southeast corner was George Buck's Ford
agency housed in a building owned by the Tilden Estate.
Across the street, Buck ran his used-car business on a site
that was ideal for a parking lot. On the northeast corner
stood yet another large building housing an auto dealer. The
buildings were all structurally sound, and they contained
large open spaces that could be developed for retail shops.
Most important, the neighborhood around Grand was one of
the most densely populated in the city. The level of education was high, and the income level was well above the city
average.The fire that had occurred had not changed any of
these factors for Jim. He still wanted to construct his vision
of a small-scale urban mall. If his partners were no longer
interested in developing a mall at Victoria Crossing, Wengler
decided he would buy them out and do the project himself.

If he could buy the body-shop/garage, which was
behind and separated from the west building by a short alley,
Wengler thought, he could roof over the short alley between
them and join the two buildings together into one big enough
to house an urban mall. The garage had once been a livery
stable serving the houses on Summit Avenue. There were
still grooves in the concrete floor to facilitate hosing it down
and vestiges of feeding stations still in the walls.

The body shop was leased to George Buck, who used
it to repair the cars he sold from his Ford agency and the used
cars he sold in the lot across the street. Buck was ready to
retire, and the Tilden estate agreed to sell the garage. Again
Clapp Thomssen was the realtor. Jim and the realtor wrote

up a purchase agreement for the body shop for $48,000, and the realtor went on vacation. When he returned, he found that someone else in the company had gone ahead and sold the body shop to Jim Hulfman from the Crocus Hill market. Wenglers's dream to build an urban mall at Grand and Victoria was to be no more than a dream unless he could get the body shop building back from Hulfman. Wengler did, but at a price. He had to buy it back from Hulfman for $60,000.

Wengler also needed a parking lot if he was going to have a mall, even a small urban mall. The empty lot on the southwest corner of the street was owned by Buck. There was a small building at the back of the lot where the cars were washed and another where agents met with potential buyers. Originally there had been three houses on the property, facing on Victoria Street, with the used car lot occupying a smaller space behind them. Over the years, Buck had bought two of the houses to gain more room for his used-car business, but the owner of the third had refused all of Buck's offers to buy his house. Buck was so persistent that the owner became angry and refused to sell his house to Buck for any price. The matter was resolved when Buck convinced a realtor to purchase the house for him as his agent without disclosing who the real buyer was. Once Buck owned the house, he tore it down and created the parking lot. Wengler talked George Buck into leasing the lot to him with an option to buy it at some later time.

Buying out his partners exhausted all of Jim Wengler's resources. He had to put a second mortgage on his house and borrow money from an aunt to complete the deal. Then he began shopping around for permanent financing to remodel his building. The $60,000 for the body shop and a construction loan came from the First Bank Grand, but that was all they would lend. Neither the First National Bank or Norwest Bank nor any other bank would consider permanent financing for building on Grand. As Wengler remarked, "They would rather invest in condos in Florida than in property in St. Paul. Whole neighborhoods were red lined."

Wengler went from one lending institution to another in his search for financing for Victoria Crossing. Finally he found two small insurance companies, Minister's Life Insurance Company in Minneapolis and Rural Security out of Madison, Wisconsin. Together they committed to a permanent loan of $375,000. With First Bank Grand providing the $60,000 for the body shop building and the construction money and the permanent financing coming from the insurance companies, work began on the first Victoria Crossing building. The project eventually was to cost almost $500,000 with the addition of air conditioning. The insurance companies and the First Bank Grand extended their loans to cover the additional costs.

Even though work had begun, officials in St. Paul had difficulty understanding what Wengler was trying to do. In his model of the building, he had put lights on the parkway to create a welcoming ambiance and to encourage pedestrians to stroll the avenue. When Jim called the city lighting engineer to talk about installing decorative lights on the parkway in front of Victoria Crossing, the engineer was totally against it. The property belonged to the city, he said, and private citizens could not put decorative lights on city property.

Wengler thought about it a while and decided to go ahead anyway. He used workers from Fellowship Club (a halfway house run by the Hazelden Foundation) to dig up the parkway. A friend, Russ Weaver, a high school mathematics teacher, acted as foreman. The men put down conduit for the street lighting according to the city code and hoped to get it installed before anyone from the city would notice what was happening. While the project was underway, Wengler happened to be walking down Grand toward the building when he saw the city lighting engineer pull up to the site of the work in a city truck. Wengler just kept on walking. The engineer accosted Weaver, who was leaning on his shovel. "What's going on here?" he asked. "Don't know," replied Weaver. "We're just digging." The city engineer did not pursue the question further, and, once he drove off, the workers redoubled their efforts and installed the lights. Another city inspector later checked the lights for city code compliance. They passed inspection and were left in place.[4]

While construction on the building was underway, Wengler built a model of his new building and began the task of leasing it out. His old partner, Roger Swardson, wrote an article about it for the *Grand Gazette*. One of the readers of that article was a man named Tim Murphy. Tim had been a member of the wedding party of a young couple, Dan and Michelle Odegard, and, when Murphy went to visit them in Pennsylvania, he took a clipping of the article along with him.

Dan and Michelle were originally from Minnesota, he from Anoka and she from Rochester. They had met in college and were managing a bookstore in Harrisburg. The Odegards were intrigued by the newspaper clipping, by Jim's ideas, by the concept of a small urban retail setting for a

Odegard Books, December 1980. (*Highland Villager* photo.)

shopping center instead of the usual sprawling suburban malls. Despite the fact that there were already three bookstores on the street, Learn Me, Macalester Park, and the Hungry Mind, the Odegards believed the demographics and level of education of the residents of the Grand Avenue neighborhood could support another full-service bookstore.

Inspired by the newspaper article, Dan and Michelle flew out to St. Paul, met with Wengler and, in two days, as Michelle says, "got it all done." Wengler introduced them to Donald Dick, president of the First Bank Grand, who agreed to finance the bookstore. They signed a letter of intent with Jim, authorizing him to get the construction work started and, on April 17, 1978, opened their bookstore. They decided to give the business their own name, Odegard, to indicate to their customers that theirs was an independent book store. The goal was to become an excellent neighborhood book store. Within two years the store drew customers not just from the neighborhood but the entire metropolitan area.[5]

Other early tenants of Victoria Crossing West were Garuda, a Philippine restaurant, Garden of Eden, Kit Con-

Patio of Bill Wengler's American Bar and Grill. (*Highland Villager* photo.)

nection, the Crocus Hill Drugstore, Coffee & Tea Limited, Clothes to Boot, and Briar Patch, a children's clothing store. The building was fully leased and crowded with shoppers and diners from the day it opened.

Even before the west mall opened, Jim had negotiated an option to buy the building across the street on the northeast corner, which was to become Victoria Crossing East, from Rod Baxter who had a Saab agency in the building. When Baxter went out of business in 1977, Wengler, together with his brother, Bill, negotiated to buy the building. Financing for the second Victoria Crossing building came from Farmers and Mechanics Bank of Minneapolis, which took the lead position, with smaller positions held by the First Bank Grand and Western State Bank. The total cost was $750,000.

Victoria Crossing parking lot with the opera building (later Victoria Crossing South) in the background. The upper third of the building is sheathed in blue plastic panels, and the windows are covered with plywood. (David Lanegran photo.)

Recognizing how crucial parking would be to the success of the Crossing, the Farmers and Mechanics bank would agree to finance the project only if Wengler purchased the parking lot on the southwest corner and give the bank an easement on it. The fact that Wengler was leasing the lot from Buck was not enough to satisfy the bank—they required an easement. The First Bank Grand was willing to finance the purchase of the parking lot, but only if Jim sold Victoria Crossing West to reduce his debt load. Wengler had reached his lending limit, and the bank would not, or could not, bring in another participant in the project.

Jim faced a dilemma. He could not get his money from the Farmers and Mechanics Bank to finance Victoria Crossing East without purchasing the parking lot on the southwest corner, and he could not raise the money to buy the parking lot without selling something. So he sold Victoria Crossing West to a recently formed husband and wife development company, Jim Crockeral and Laurel March, who themselves soon had a falling out amid a flurry of lawsuits.

Simultaneous with the development of Victoria Crossing East, Jim formed a partnership with his brother Bill Wengler and Russ Weaver to buy the old Schiller's supermarket building at 695 Grand from Curt Carlson. The First Bank Grand again provided the construction loan, but this time the relationship was not a good one. The contractor and Henry Olson, vice-president of the First Bank, did not get along. And the timing was poor. This was during the real estate recession of the early 1980s when interest rates began to go up, eventually topping at twenty-one percent. Wengler was paying four points over prime to First Bank, at one time paying twenty-six percent interest. Wengler claims that he paid more in interest to the bank on the construction loan than the total cost of the building plus the remodeling.

Though the building was fully leased out to two restaurants, Esteban's, a Mexican restaurant and Saji Ya, a Japanese eatery, rents would not cover operating expenses and debt service because of the high interest rate. Wengler had to have a rate no higher than fourteen percent for the building to break even, and he was paying over twenty. No lender would give him a lower rate of interest because of the interest rate environment of those years. Finally, unable to find partners to help him with the financing, he was forced to sell the building. To his astonishment, according to Jim, the First Bank Grand, while refusing Wengler a loan of fourteen percent on the project, financed it at thirteen percent for Emmett Kennifack so that he could buy out Wengler and his partners.

The fourth piece in Wengler's plan for the Victoria Crossing area was the building on the southeast corner of the intersection. It, too, was in the Tilden Estate and had been sold to the Minnesota Opera Company. Jim went to the director of the opera company and negotiated a deal. In exchange for free parking for the opera company trucks and cars in the parking lot, the director would give Jim first option on the purchase of the opera company building. Believing his option was secure, Jim had turned his attention to the building at 695 Grand. Unfortunately, the director of the opera company left for another job and neglected to tell anyone about the option he had negotiated with Wengler in exchange for free parking. A fire broke out in the building, the opera company decided it needed more space, and before Jim realized what was happening or could do anything about it, the opera building had been sold to another developer, Howard Bergerud.

Wengler's dream of building a unified urban mall at the intersection of Grand and Victoria on his own had been frustrated. He felt that the local bank had done its best to see that he would not be successful He was down to one building on Grand, Victoria Crossing East, which he owned in partnership with his brother Bill. In disgust, and because of this experience and other problem properties in downtown St. Paul and Rochester, Jim Wengler gave up on Grand Avenue, moved out of town and took up residence on his sailboat in the Caribbean.

Notes

1. James Wengler and Roger Swardson.

2. Interview by Billie Young with James Stolpestad, November 4, 1995. Stolpestad remembers that when Kohner and Fredric were asked to vacate the building, Stolpestad's neighbor, Beth McGrath, came over to his house on Saturday morning to protest the decision. People in the neighborhood were beginning to show concern about what happened on Grand.

3. Jim Wengler wanted the enlarged sidewalk to be made of brick not cement. Jim Stolpestad was dispatched to visit the St. Paul director of Public Works, Dan Dunford, to ask for permission to put down a brick sidewalk. The plan was vetoed by Dunford, who told Stolpestad that the city would allow only concrete sidewalks.

4. Jim Wengler, July 6, 1995.

5. Interview by Billie Young with Michele Poire Cromer, May 31, 1995.

12

First Bank Grand:
The Uneasy Partner

Jim Wengler's sometimes reluctant partner throughout his years of building on Grand Avenue was Donald Dick, president of First Bank Grand. While conceding that their relationship was frequently stormy, Dick gives Wengler most of the credit for the development and success of Grand Avenue. "He had the vision," said Dick. "And our problems were not anybody's fault. It was the times."[1]

Dick came to the First Bank Grand as vice president in 1968, moving into the presidency in 1972. A native of Mountain View, Minnesota, and a World War II veteran (a radioman on a navy munitions ship in the Pacific), Dick came into the Grand Avenue bank determined to find good loans. Deposits came easily, but finding good loans was hard, especially on Grand Avenue. The bank made many automobile loans (reflecting the presence of the car dealers on Grand) and boat loans, but Dick was looking for something more. He and his staff at the bank identified strongly with Grand Avenue and the neighborhood, considering it their territory, and they wanted to influence what happened there. When Dick looked at the neighborhood, he saw past the blight on Grand to its strengths—the solid residential area, Summit Avenue, and Macalester College. "If you don't have a good neighborhood," said Dick, "you have to work to create it." The bank got its chance when Wengler and his partners created Victoria Crossing.

Dick had first met Wengler when the bank began

participating in rehabilitation projects in the historic preservation area north of Summit, an area where Wengler was also deeply involved. On his first Grand Avenue project, the combining of the building on the northwest corner of Grand and Victoria with the body-shop/garage to create the first Victoria Crossing, the costs began to run higher than the estimate. Jim had planned to spend about $350,000, but he kept adding amenities, such as air conditioning, and the costs escalated. Dick, who had provided the construction loan, took deep breaths and hung on.

When the Victoria Crossing East project began, Dick made sure that the Grand Avenue bank participated, signaling to other businesses that, while First Bank Grand could not take the lead role in the project because Wengler was at his lending limit, it was involved. This demonstrated to other lending institutions that Grand Avenue was First Bank Grand territory.

The bank conveyed that message in an even more definite fashion. Information circulated within the banking community that a rival bank planned to move onto Grand Avenue and construct a building on a certain lot on the street. Dick learned of it through the banking grapevine and quickly lent money to another non-banking business to build on the proposed site.

The bank's attempt to solve what it perceived to be its parking problem, coupled with its attitude that it could do what it wanted on the street, embroiled the bank in two major conflicts with the Grand Avenue community. The first was the demolition of the venerable Uptown Theater.

The bank believed that it had a critical parking problem and that it could not grow without additional spaces for cars. The noon hour had become a busy time for the bank, and there were not enough places, in the bank's opinion, for customers to park to transact their bank business. Noon was also a busy time for the Lexington Restaurant across the street, and customers for the two institutions, between them, absorbed much of the available parking. Without additional parking, the bank feared, its customers would go elsewhere. Not only would present customers be unhappy, but the organization would not be able to attract additional accounts and expand. The Uptown Theater, two buildings east of the bank, stood empty. For $45,000, the bank bought it to tear down and pave the area for a parking lot.

When word reached the community that a local landmark, the Uptown Theater, was going to be torn down, many residents complained. Women pushing baby buggies

114

The Uptown Theater before it was demolished by First Bank Grand to provide parking for twenty-four cars. (Photo courtesy of David Lanegran.)

conducted an informal traffic count on the block in an attempt to convince the bank that the existing parking was adequate. The president of the Summit Hill Association wrote a letter opposing the proposed demolition. Elberta Matters, the editor of the *Grand Gazette*, rallied support for the theater. She went so far as to find a buyer for the building who wanted to convert it into shops on the order of Victoria Crossing. Unfortunately, her efforts only reinforced the bank's decision to tear down the theater. While the bank was not against retail business on Grand, it did not want more retail in its block because it would only add to the parking problem.

In August 1977, a wrecking ball smashed into the Uptown Theater. Demolition of the building and the construction of the parking lot eventually cost the bank three to four times the cost of the theater. The sloping floor of the theater had been built of very thick, solid concrete. The old Uptown Theater proved to be one of the sturdiest buildings in St. Paul.

Many people grieved to see the building go to gain twenty-four parking spaces. Representative Fred Norton, now a Minnesota State Court of Appeals judge, wrote an angry letter to the *Grand Gazette* and, the day the building went down, closed his accounts at First Bank Grand.[2]

The parking spaces gained by the removal of the Uptown Theater did not solve the bank's parking problem, however, and Dick made inquiries of the bank's neighbors. One of them, Platt Walker, owned a house on Summit Avenue directly behind and across the alley from the Grand Avenue bank. Platt sold a strip of his land forty feet deep by

First Bank Grand's parking lot on the site of the Uptown Theater. The mural on the side of the Bober Drug building, commissioned by the bank, is by Chris Baird. (Dave Lanegran photo.)

121 feet long along the alley to First Bank Grand. At the time the bank bought the land, Dick knew that he could not legally use the strip for parking, though it would hold about a dozen cars. The bank's attorney had thoroughly researched the various covenants restricting land use around Summit Avenue and advised that it could not be used to park cars.

Dick countered that the bank could use the land on which to pile snow during the winter. The hauling away of snow was a major expense for the bank, and, if he could simply bulldoze the snow onto the newly acquired strip, Dick would save the bank money. Then, if anyone were to park on the strip in the summer, Dick would not have them towed. While Dick was president of the bank, the strip was never blacktopped, no signs were ever put up, no stripes painted to indicate that it could be used as a parking lot. It was simply a strip of empty land along the alley behind the bank. Nevertheless, customers and employees of the bank quickly found it, and it was soon filled with automobiles.

For a couple of years, the bank's unofficial parking lot escaped the scrutiny of the Summit Hill Association and the Summit Avenue Residential Preservation Association. By the time it came to their attention, Don Dick had retired, and Pat Crowns was the president of First Bank Grand. The strip had been covered with asphalt and parking signage installed. The illegality of the parking use was brought to the bank's attention by the two neighborhood groups, and a protracted process of negotiation took place over a two-year period of time during which feelings ran high on both sides of the issue. The final settlement allowed the bank to keep the property and use it for parking for a period of ten years, ending in 2001. During those ten years, the bank was to dispose of the strip. In the meantime, the city initiated a zoning text amendment to allow the bank lot to become a legal nonconforming space.[3] The dispute left a residue of bitterness about parking, much of which was a result of the hubris of earlier years. As Don Dick remarked about the land purchase, "We knew at the time what we were getting into."

The lawlessness that afflicted Grand Avenue in the early 1970s also hit First Bank Grand. In 1970, a gang of four or five people, waving shotguns, yelling and screaming, charged into the bank, terrorized the staff and customers and escaped with a sum of money. The bank robbers forced the people in the bank, including Dick, to lie on the floor while they collected the money from the tellers. While the money was never recovered, the gang was later apprehended in another midwestern city after a similar robbery.

Two years later, Dick was on the telephone with Max Lein, president of the Minnesota Museum of Art, when he looked out the glass window of his office and saw a similar scene. "We are being robbed," he said to Lein over the phone. "How do you know?" Lein asked. "Because I can see my secretary down on the floor," answered Dick. Dick hung up, and Lein called the police.[4]

One bank teller, Lucille Fohlmeister, who had been on duty during the first bank robbery, saw the second gang come into the bank. She immediately scooped up the money from her teller's drawer and dumped it in the waste basket.

One day a would-be bank robber came into the bank by himself. He handed a note demanding money to teller Bertha Koch. Koch calmly read the note, looked up at the robber and said, "No." The man turned and left.

Dick met some of his loan recipients in unusual ways. When developer John Rupp was a student in law school, he happened to be in the bank when a group of youth ripped out a handful of pens from the bank tables and ran out of the door with them. Tellers shouted, and Rupp chased after the youth, collaring two of them and bringing them back to the bank. A few years later, Dick financed W. A. Frost, Rupp's restaurant and redevelopment project on Selby Avenue.

The First Bank Grand, under Don Dick, grew from a bank with thirty million dollars in assets to a $130-million institution. Profits increased six fold from the time when he started. Dick retired from the bank in the winter of 1984 after thirty-five years of service with the First Bank system.

The Milton Mall at Grand
Avenue and Milton Street.
(Dave Lanegran photo.)

Notes

1. Interview by Billie Young with Don Dick, July 17, 1995.

2. *Grand Gazette*, letter to the editor from Fred Norton, August, 1977 , p. 4. In his letter, Judge Norton wrote, "Part of the reason I particularly deplore the action is that the detached banking facilities bill was acted on favorably in this past legislative session. I believe that you misled the Summit Hill community in implying that this was a major factor in your decision whether or not to demolish the theater building. I am very sorry that you could not use the legislation as you had indicated you might."

3. Interview by Billie Young with Chris Trost, July 26, 1995.

4. Don Dick.

13

Mary Rice and Her Grand Old Ideas

IN ADDITION TO THE Old Mexico Shop and the Victoria Crossing developments, a third small business on the street had an impact far beyond what could be expected from its size. That business was Thrice—a cookware store and later a cooking school—founded in May 1973 in a tiny space at 1086½ Grand Avenue by Mary Rice, her sister Martha Kaemmer, and Steve Soderman. The business was to be of enormous significance to the future of the street because of the creativity of the owners, particularly that of Mary Rice.

Mary Rice saw Grand Avenue not just as a collection of small shops and businesses competing with one another but as a three-mile-long shopping experience. She thought that the avenue should be promoted as a friendly neighborhood unit with shoppers encouraged to walk from store to store. Businesses should cooperate with one another as well as engage in competition. That Christmas, searching for a way to promote the street, Mary and Roger Swardson suggested that businesses stage a "Grand Meander" on the first Saturday in December to encourage shoppers to patronize all the businesses on Grand. The name of the event carried the idea of strolling the avenue, and, even though the weather in December was seldom conducive to walking very far, the event captured the neighborhood's imagination.

Roger Swardson used his great supply of Victorian steel engraving clip art for advertising the event. Mary promoted an image of chestnuts roasting on open fires along the street. She convinced a number of stores to adopt a Dicken-

119

Mary Rice as the 1978 Grand Marshall of the Grand Old Day parade. The Thrice store and Cooking School are in the background. (Stephen Soderman photo.)

Lea Kling of Cooks of Crocus Hill serves chestnuts at the 1993 Grand Meander. (*Highland Villager* photo.)

sonian theme for the event and to offer a roasted chestnut (or a cup of hot cider) to every customer who came to the Grand Meander. Many stores did. The Old Mexico Shop owners brought their charcoal grills from home, set them up in the snow on the sidewalk and roasted chestnuts on the coals. Unfortunately they did not know that chestnuts had to have an X cut into their skins before roasting. The uncut chestnuts exploded as they roasted, splattering hot chestnuts on the street, the shop windows, and in the hands and faces of customers who had come to participate in the avenue's first Grand Meander.

Merrie Olde Christmas Carolers singing at the Bibelot Shop, Grand Meander, 1991. (*Highland Villager* photo.)

FREE HAYRIDES
NOON TO 4TH

Hayrides on Grand Meander near Dale Street. (*Highland Villager* photo.)

Mary Rice's second idea began as a benefit for Children's Hospital. In the spring of 1974, she was chairman of an event she called "Grand Old Day." Stores on Grand Avenue were asked to stay open on a Sunday afternoon in June, and the public was invited to walk the avenue, buy food from a handful of food venders on the street and visit the few sidewalk booths set up by the shops. It was the Grand Meander with warm weather. For organizing the event and providing help and publicity, the hospital was to receive ten percent of the sales. As Mary said, "We needed a street fair, and small business owners didn't have time to run one by themselves. By doing it with Children's Hospital, we gained both a noble purpose and volunteers."[1] Mary Rice, members of her committee, which included Mary Wilson and Billie Young from the Old Mexico Shop, and Children's Hospital volunteers walked the avenue talking business owners into staying open that Sunday afternoon and participating in an observance they were calling Grand Old Day.

The first Grand Old Day dawned sunny and clear. The Old Mexico Shop and a few others had set up tables on the sidewalk. The Old Mexico tables were shaded by a bedsheet, held up by tent poles, to simulate a Mexican market stall. Children's Hospital volunteers set up a popcorn stand beside the stall in the other half of the driveway of the auto body shop. Several hundred people walked the avenue that day, and about fifty visited the shop and the popcorn stand.

After the first few Grand Old Days, the event was taken over by the Grand Avenue Business Association and run as a benefit for Grand Avenue. The event was a pleasant annual occurrence, billed as a homecoming for friends of the avenue and an opportunity to return and visit favorite old haunts. The parade was an occasion for fun. A group of young mothers organized a stroller brigade and did elaborate maneuvers with their children in the parade. Their husbands performed routines with their power lawn mowers. The bars'

Jazz fusion band, "Higher Ground," Grand Old Day 1987. (*Highland Villager* photo.)

122

participation was largely limited to the provision of waiters and waitresses for the "Waiters Olympics," a race down the avenue with trays of filled glasses. The event drew a few thousand people every June, until the end of the 1970s when it suddenly exploded.

Under the direction of an all-volunteer committee and later of Mimi Doran, executive director of the Grand Avenue Business Association, attendance leaped from the hundreds to the hundreds of thousands. For one Sunday afternoon in June, tens of thousands of people come from as far away as Wisconsin and Iowa to walk the three miles of Grand Avenue, listen to bands in almost every block, watch the parade, dine on a vast assortment of foods, drink beer and lemonade and see their neighbors.

Aris Apostolou and his wife Cassandra, owners of the Acropole Restaurant at 748 Grand, typically stay up all night on the night before Grand Old Day. After closing their restaurant at 10:00 P.M. they begin the slow roasting of fifteen lambs on the street in front of their restaurant. By morning the fragrance of roasted lamb drifts over the neighborhood, and, by the time the crowds descend on the street, Aris, Cassandra, their children, and staff busily carve the meat into hundreds of Gyros sandwiches. They end the day doing Greek dances in big hand-holding circles on the street until the slow-cruising police cars close down the celebration at 5:00 P.M.[2]

For twelve years running, the Rockin' Hollywoods band played in the Kowalski grocery store parking lot on Grand Old Day, and groups of fans staged their annual reunions to coincide with the event. A motorcycle group, whose members happened to like the Rockin' Hollywoods interpretation of music from the 1960s, came every year. On the tenth anniversary of their appearance, they rode in the Grand Old Day parade as grand marshals.[3]

Kowalski's Market at 1261 Grand Avenue. (Dave Lanegran photo.)

In 1983, Matt McDonough of Grand Spectacle was the volunteer in charge of the art fair held at Macalester College in conjunction with Grand Old Day. He got up at 4:00 A.M. of the big day with a pocket full of chalk and a ruler to measure off and mark the spaces on the street that would be occupied by the participants in the art fair. He was meticulous in measuring and drawing his lines. He had barely finished when a brief but heavy shower wiped out all his work, and, when the street had dried, he had to start all over again.

The following year, Nancy Fish of Bywords Printing was chairman of the art fair. Remembering Matt's misfortune, she bought some cans of washable spray paint and lined

The Rockin' Hollywoods performing in Kowalski's Market parking lot. (*Highland Villager* photo.)

Bob Kowalski eating a turkey leg at Grand Old Day 1991. (*Highland Villager* photo.)

up friends to help her draw lines. Unfortunately, the friends failed to appear. At 10:30 P.M. on the night before Grand Old Day, Nancy was out on Grand Avenue on her hands and knees painting lines on the street. Two policeman and a security guard from Macalester challenged her. She finish the job about 2:00 A.M. on the morning of Grand Old Day.[4]

In 1985, the entire Grand Old Day central committee consisted of Jim and Jeannine Solen, Irene DeVinney, Mike Mischke, and Nancy Fish. They decided to provide heavy plastic reusable beer mugs as a way to both raise money for the association and cut down on the volume of trash generated by the festival. They took orders from Grand Old Day venders, who agreed to sell the mugs, and a total of ninety-six cases of mugs were ordered and delivered to Bywords Printing for distribution to venders on Grand Old Day. The mugs sold well, so, the next year, the committee decided to do it again and reordered ninety-six more cases of mugs.

The day before Grand Old Day arrived, and the mugs had not been delivered. They had gotten lost in shipping. Nancy traced them from the factory in New Jersey to Atlanta, Georgia, to Chicago. There they would stay unless someone came for them. Nancy hired a friend with a jeep and a flatbed trailer to drive all night to Chicago and pick up the mugs. At 8:00 A.M. on the morning of Grand Old Day, the exhausted friend appeared in Nancy's driveway with the mugs. He and Nancy raced down Grand Avenue, distributing the mugs to the venders just before the crowds descended on the street.

In 1986, Harvey Geise and his wife were in charge of the parade, and the line-up started at Dale Street and backed up all the way down the hill. The entries spread out all the way to West Seventh. Nancy Fish was a volunteer working on the parade and wore herself out running up and down the hill checking in the participants and lining them up for the parade. The next year, when she became parade chairman (a position she was to hold for seven years) she moved the beginning of the parade up two blocks to cut out at least part of the hill. During her years as parade chairman, Nancy coped with hissing llamas who refused to move, two monster oxen, Barney and Brutus, who splattered a golf cart and its passengers, Jerry Payne and Mike Mischke, who had steered too close at a critical moment, and found socks for a sockless member of a marching band.

Grand Old Day crowds. (*Highland Villager* photo.)

In 1988, when Bill Crum was parade co-chair with Nancy, a company called Natural Ovens located north of Milwaukee, Wisconsin, called and asked to bring their horse-drawn bread wagon to drive in the parade. Nancy and Bill had no sooner said, "Yes," when the owner added that he would need some place to house his horses overnight on the night before the parade. Nancy had a small mare and an elderly paint horse penned in a small enclosure next to her house in Inver Grove Heights, so she offered to take the horses for the night. To her astonishment, the evening before Grand Old Day, a semi truck pulling an enormous horse trailer arrived at her door and unloaded four massive Belgian draft horses. The animals were led into the lot with Nancy's mare, who took one look at the handsome visiting horses and began to prance and flirt. The aging paint perceived the Belgians as unwelcome competition. All night the six horses snorted, pawed the ground and chased each other around the tiny lot while Nancy tried to sleep above the din.

There were never enough convertibles for the parade. Brian Valento of Grand Avenue Frame and Gallery offered his one year, and the committee put a pretty girl from one of the clothing stores in the car. As the day heated up, the girl began to take off her clothes, ending up in the skimpiest bikini anyone on Grand Avenue had ever seen. Letters to the editor of the *Gazette* and phone calls to the parade chairman followed that exhibition.

Grand Old Day and the parade are still wonderfully unsophisticated. The mayor rides in the parade on a fire

Bouncing girl, Grand Old Day 1990. (*Highland Villager* photo.)

Briefcase Brigade from Caldwell Banker, Grand Old Day 1994. (*Highland Villager* photo.)

truck. There are high school marching bands, harvest queens, and the Winter Carnival Royalty. The Caldwell Bankers drill team of real estate agents in their suits and with briefcases go through their maneuvers for the crowd, and a girl is tossed high on a blanket. Dale Wildmo of the Tavern on Grand turns his car into a twenty-five-foot-long walleye fish with an undulating tail for the parade. There are no extremes, no semi-nude walkers, few drunks.

The remarkable thing about Grand Old Day is how benign the day is. More than a quarter of a million people crowd onto the street for six hours, and there are few serious problems. The police cannot believe how little trouble there is. One man bent a pole climbing it to get a better view of the parade, and another dented the hood of a car for the same reason. A few people use the alleys for bathrooms. The only disaster was the year when a sign tied to a defective light pole turned into a sail and pulled the light pole over onto a spectator. The Grand Avenue Business Association and the city of St. Paul were sued. The person who put up the sign, Dede Wozniac from Hobbit Travel, was not. Otherwise, nothing bad happened on Grand Old Day.[5]

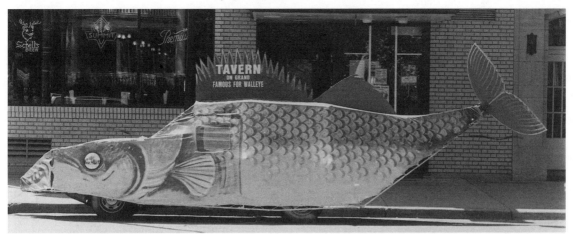

Walleye float from the Tavern on Grand. (*Highland Villager* photo.)

One of the committee's biggest problems relating to Grand Old Day was that of gypsy vendors. Salesmen of food and souvenirs who had not been authorized by the Grand Old Day committee would come to the street on Grand Old Day and set up shop anywhere they chose. The city had not given the Grand Avenue Business Association authority to keep them off the street for the day but yet insisted that the association take responsibility for them. The solution would be the passage by the city council of a block-party ordinance. The committee lobbied for several years to pass such an ordinance but got little help from the business people on the street who, once Grand Old Day was over, turned their attention to other business concerns.

Then, on Grand Old Day in 1987, a gypsy ice cream vendor set up his stand directly in front of the Häagen-Dazs ice cream store owned by Peter Quinn at Grand and Victoria. This quickly got Quinn's attention. He immediately got behind the block party ordinance, and it was passed in 1990.[6]

The celebration has benefited from an amazing string of days with good weather. Year after year, the sun would shine, and the temperature would hover in the low eighties for Grand Old Day. The fame of Grand Old Day continued to spread. In 1989, *US News and World Report* listed it as one of the major travel destinations in the country and *INC Magazine*, based in Boston, Massachusetts, sent a reporter to write a major story about the street.

In 1990, the date for Grand Old Day coincided with the day the premier of the Soviet Union, Mikhail Gorbachev, and his wife were scheduled to visit St. Paul. Moreover, the Russian guests were to have lunch with Governor Rudy Perpich at the governor's official residence on Summit

Grand Old Day crowds. (*Highland Villager* photo.)

127

Avenue, just one block from the thousands of revelers of Grand Old Day. Gorbachev's advance team called Grand Avenue Association Business Executive Mimi three months before the event and asked her to change the date for Grand Old Day. Mimi refused, and volunteer parade chairman Nancy Fish wrote a letter to Moscow inviting Gorbachev to ride in the parade as grand marshall.

Nancy never received a reply to her letter. The Grand Old Day committee would not change its date for the event, and Gorbachev's planners could not change their date for the visit, so the two events were forced to coexist. Mimi and members of her committee were briefed by the police and the secret service and were taught how to look for bombs. As it turned out, Grand Old Day provided no security threat to the premier, though security was much in evidence. On the morning of Grand Old Day, Mimi was driving her golf cart down the alley behind the governor's mansion when the cart backfired. Heads popped up from all the roof tops, guns in hand, to see what had made the noise.

The biggest problem for the 1990 Grand Old Day turned out to be, not the Russian premier, but the weather. Instead of a warm sunny day, as had occurred for more than a dozen years, the weather turned cold. Mike Mischke, editor of the *Grand Gazette* and volunteer in charge of the children's area that year, had a sidewalk parade down Grand planned. The afternoon turned out to be so cold that Mike called the janitor at Ramsey Junior High School, who opened the gymnasium for him. Mike took the children inside and paraded them around and around the gym.

The children's parade ran into problems again in 1991. That year 200 children, all in costume, turned out for the parade, which was to be led by Ronald McDonald of Ronald McDonald House fame. The children were all lined

Enjoying Grand Old Day at the Johnson McClay Law Office. (*Highland Villager* photo.)

Eating ice cream bars on Grand Old Day. (*Highland Villager* photo.)

up behind a rope barricade ready to march, but Ronald did not appear. He had failed to grasp the enormity of Grand Old Day and had tried to drive down Grand to the parade starting point only to find 100,000 people blocking his way. When McDonald did not appear, Tom Larson, co-chair of the children's area, thought briefly of squeezing himself into the Panda costume used by the Teddy Bear Band and leading the parade himself. With 200 children straining at the ropes, no time could be lost. Nancy and Tom gave up on Ronald McDonald, still lost in the crowd, and themselves led the children in their annual parade down Grand.

Mary Rice's original idea for Grand Old Day was to market the street to the community as a unit. Her idea succeeded beyond everyone's expectations. Grand Old Day is now the largest one-day festival in the Upper Midwest. It is run completely by volunteers, with the exception of the staff person from the Grand Avenue Business Association, and planning for the event goes on all year. Volunteers spend countless hours in meetings on the avenue, meetings with the city, organizing volunteers, assembling street barricades,

Grand Old Day Committee 1989. Back row: Mike Mischke, Bob McClay, Adrian Stetler, Scott LaValle, Jim Rouleau, Nancy Fish, Dirk Dantuma, and Jerry Payne. Front row: Mella Martin, Bill McCrum, Mimi Doran, and Tony Gagliardi. The picture was taken on the roof of the First Bank Grand. (*Highland Villager* photo.)

negotiating and assigning spaces to street venders, serving beer on the day itself, lining up the parade, putting together trash boxes, filling gift bags for children, and cleaning up after everyone else has gone home. The Friday before the event is spent putting up street signs along the entire three miles of the avenue.

After complaints by some in the neighborhood that the event was becoming too large and getting out of hand, more control of beer stands and of the decibel level of the bands was instituted. Instead of allowing revelers to walk along the street, beer in hand, they are now confined within snow fences erected in the parking lots around the principal purveyors of beer. Residents of the Summit Hill neighborhood have served on the most recent Grand Old Day committees along with members of the business association.

It would be hard to overestimate the benefit of Grand Old Day to the business community on Grand Avenue. Dick Swinney of Our Gang Hair Designs, is still fixing the hair of three customers he got on his first Grand Old Day in 1976.[7] Steve Lyon, of Lyon's Pub at 788 Grand Avenue, calls it "the best marketing tool I have ever seen," and believes, "the avenue would never have developed as it has if it had not been for Grand Old Day." A Minneapolis resident, Lyon learned about Grand Avenue because of the publicity generated by the event, and, when he was looking for a location for his business, he investigated the street. He says it was the only street in St. Paul he would have considered.[8] Because of Grand Old Day, Grand Avenue has become more than a main street of St. Paul, it has become a street that is claimed as their own by residents throughout the entire metropolitan area.

Notes

1. Telephone interview by Billie Young with Mary Rice, July 29, 1995.

2. Interview by Billie Young with Aris and Cassandra Apostolou, October 13, 1995.

3. Interview by Billie Young with Mike Mischke, May 31, 1995.

4. Interview by Billie Young with Nancy Fish, August 21, 1995.

5. Mike Mischke.

6. Interview by Billie Young with Mimi Doran, October 10, 1994.

7. Interview by Billie Young with Dick Swinney, September 14, 1995.

8. Interview by Billie Young with Steve Lyon, August 21, 1995.

14

The Great Battle over Zoning

ONE OF THE MOST SIGNIFICANT governmental decisions affecting the resurgence of Grand Avenue was that of land-use zoning. The city's right to control land use comes from the police power that is reserved to the state governments. In order to protect the health and welfare of the population, the state government gave cities the right to restrict land use without having to pay any compensation to the landowners. In theory, land should be used for what will bring in the most money, or the "highest and best use." But zoning frequently prevented owners from developing land for the greatest profit because to do so would conflict with the public welfare.

In reality, because many land uses affect the quality of the environment around them, it was realized that a blind application of the highest and best use test, or unbridled use of property, would, in many cases, reduce the safety and value of property nearby. As industrial cities grew during the boom period of the 1890s, the need for some sort of regulation of land use became increasingly apparent. Several methods based on deeds and contracts for sale of property were used to protect high income residential districts. But these processes did not work for the people who lived in middle- and working-class neighborhoods.

The ideas of sociologists and urban ecologists were an important part of the discussions around zoning. Almost everyone felt that some form of control was needed to protect neighborhoods from rapid invasion by commercial and industrial uses that had the potential to destroy urban communities. Zoning laws were a solution but a controversial one. Proponents of zoning were taken to court by land owners, but the zoning laws survived several court challenges. The courts held that, as long as a comprehensive plan guided the over-all pattern of land use and as long as the zoning and rezoning process was not capricious, landowners must abide by its regulation.

Zoning first came to St. Paul in 1922, soon after the idea of zoning was developed. In that first zoning law, the categories of land use were broad and included commercial, industrial, high-density housing and low-density housing. The zoning law also contained the notion that lower order land uses could be developed in areas that were zoned for a higher use. One could build a house in an area zoned for commercial (houses were lower than commercial) because it was assumed that commercial land use would eventually replace the housing. Most of the streets with streetcar lines were zoned Commercial. Except for a few blocks of "C" Residential (apartment buildings), Grand Avenue was zoned Commercial from the Oakland intersection to Cretin Avenue, or just about its entire length.

Because St. Paul did not expand as expected, the land use pattern did not reflect the zoning map. The industrial and commercial areas did not get as big as predicted and homes were built in the commercial districts. This was especially true for Grand Avenue. Commercial land use was concentrated on corners with multiple and single family houses occupying the remainder of most blocks. There were also sections of the street with no commercial use whatsoever.

The City Planning Department and its consultants, in the late 1960s and early 1970s, recommended rezoning the entire city. They believed more categories of land use were needed to reflect the complexity of an automobile-dominated city. For example, the old plans did not take into account freeway-oriented developments, and there were many new patterns of residential densities. In general, planners believed that zoning should be consistent with what was actually happening on the land. If an activity did not conform to the new land-use regulation it would be allowed to stay where it was, but it would not be allowed to be expanded or rebuilt following a disaster, such as a fire.

City planners developed a proposed new zoning law and map and began holding public hearing on it in all parts of the city. Toward the end of the process, in 1972, they got to Grand Avenue. The planners had postponed meeting on

Grand until near the end of the process because they knew the new plans would generate controversy. Almost the full length of Grand was zoned commercial, and the new plan called for changing it to largely residential. Finally, the planners could delay no longer and called a meeting. As they had suspected, members of the Grand Avenue Business Association were opposed to the suggested rezoning, believing it would be bad for business. Moreover, they were convinced that the changes being proposed were based on an anti-business viewpoint. These were the radical years when all capitalists were suspect. Running below the surface of all the discussions was a conservative versus liberal ideological debate.

The members of the business association wanted to leave all but the western-most section of Grand zoned for business. (By this time Doc Chop had gotten the portion of Grand east of Oakland renamed Grand Hill, and it was no longer part of the debate.) The association was willing to give up the far west portion of the street because there were few members of the association out there and the area was basically residential. The leaders of the business community believed that the more businesses on the avenue the better the street would be. What was good for Grand Avenue merchants was good for the street. Furthermore, they were convinced that, if the new zoning map were to duplicate the existing land use (which was mostly houses) on Grand, all business expansion on the avenue would cease. There would be no place for it to grow. This would quickly lead to deterioration because if a business could not grow it would not survive.

The planning staff and many residents of the area saw it differently. They believed the growth of business should be controlled. "After all," they asserted, "that is what zoning is

Silver Creek Traders at 1144 Grand Avenue, an example of the reuse of a residence for a business. (Dave Lanegran photo.)

supposed to do." They did not want Grand to become a "franchise row" where fast food businesses would attract more traffic to the area and create pollution. They wanted Grand to be just a simple neighborhood shopping street.

The two positions were diametrically opposed. In the early salvos of the debate, the two sides hurled unsupported assertions at each other. Business people pointed out the size of their investment and criticized the slip-shod maintenance levels of the apartment buildings and single family houses. Residents talked about the threat of increased traffic to the growing number of children in the area.

Essentially, neither side knew what it was talking about. No one knew if businesses were profitable and wanted to expand or were just struggling and hoping to sell out. No one knew for sure how many businesses were on the avenue or from where their customers came. Nor, for that matter, was much known about the residents of the buildings along the street.

Roger Swardson, Macalester College's representative to the board of the Grand Avenue Business Association, proposed a solution that would lower the rhetoric and clarify the debate. He suggested a collaboration between the association and Macalester in which the association would contribute $500 to Macalester's Geography Department to defray the expenses of a survey and report on Grand by the Urban Geography Field Seminar. The suggestion met with approval, and the leadership of the association encouraged business owners to cooperate with the students and helped them set the research topics.

When the study, headed by Macalester Professor David Lanegran and titled *The Avenue 1973*, was completed, it revealed several startling facts and eventually led to the development of a compromise plan. The first step of the study had been to develop an accurate and detailed map of land use. While there were no great surprises in the map, the students did document the fact that there were more businesses on the street than most residents believed. And contrary to what some of the old timers on the street feared, new businesses were being attracted to Grand Ave in surprisingly large numbers.

In the spring of 1973, there were 200 businesses on the street, thirty-four or seventeen percent of which had been in business for less than five years. The presence of the new businesses indicated that change was coming. While only thirty-eight percent of the old businesses were engaged in retail, fully half of the new businesses were. The new busi-

Grand Avenue street scene. (*Highland Villager* photo.)

134

nesses clustered in two locations—between Oxford and Lexington and in the 1600 block near Macalester College. The median age of the new owners was thirty-two. One third of the new owners lived in the neighborhoods immediately adjacent to Grand Avenue, and all but one reported increasing profits.

The most telling find of the study was the growth potential of the new business. About one third had definite plans to expand at their site, and four intended to relocate off Grand Avenue because they needed more space than was available on the street. When asked why they had located on Grand, the owners responded with references to the nature of the street and the surrounding communities.[1]

Using the information on where customers lived, seminar students determined the dollars available in Grand Avenue's immediate trade area. They learned that the average family income was $16,546, well above the national average in those years. When the dollars available in the trade area were added up, it was clear that the merchants on Grand Avenue were sitting in the middle of a huge pile of money. Theirs was one of the best trade areas in the metro region. Actually, the seminar understated the size of the trade area because the students could not accurately account for the great drawing power of many of the establishments. When they found that fifty percent of the customers came from within two miles of the street, they used that distance as the trade area. However they measured it, the potential for growth on Grand Avenue was tremendous.

Several issues, however, were believed to be standing in the way of the avenue's success. Those issues were lack of parking, crime, low levels of building maintenance, lack of commercial buildings and growing competition from subur-

Ace Hardware, a traditional commercial corner at 1676 Grand Avenue. The store draws customers from a five-mile radius. (Dave Lanegran photo.)

ban malls. There were few parking lots on Grand in 1973. As to crime on Grand, the memories of past crimes and the perception of crime were greater than the actual fact. The police reported that crime on Grand was only twenty to twenty-five percent as high as the rate in the Selby-Dale grid. The street was not one of the city's targeted high-crime areas, and the crime rate had been declining even though the reporting methods were improving. The crime problem was becoming a matter of perception and tolerance level.

The most surprising finding of the study was that the business section of Grand was largely owner occupied, while the residential portions of the street were dominated by absentee landlords. This situation was the reverse of the expected pattern of land tenure. Sixty-five percent of commercial property owners had two lots or less; the only large parcels were the automobile dealerships and apartments. Seventy-one percent of the owners of commercial property also had interests in the businesses on that property.

The apartments were occupied by two very different groups, middle-class elderly and those in their twenties and early thirties. The elderly seem to have moved onto Grand from the surrounding neighborhoods, but the younger people came from all over. Many were attracted to the colleges; others wanted a convenient, inexpensive short-term residence.

Another surprising result of the study was the information on changes in incomes in the Grand Avenue trade area during the 1960s. At a time when all the experts were reporting the death of the inner cities, the census tracts making up Grand Avenue's trade area were increasing in income. The study showed that the percentage of lower-income households was decreasing and the percentage of higher-income households was increasing.

The implication of all this newly discovered data was that the outcome of the zoning argument was crucial. The potential for business community growth, though many still did not know it, was tremendous. The wrong zoning decision could destroy the vibrancy of the commercial community just when the city desperately needed more economic development. By the same token, the wrong zoning decision could have a deleterious effect on the revitalization process transforming the neighborhoods of Grand's trade area.

The Avenue 1973 was printed and distributed widely to city planners, members of the Grand Avenue Business Association and residents in the neighborhood. Armed with in-depth and up-to-date information, the protagonists were ready to face off again over the issues. The meeting was held in Doc Chop's dental office next door to the infamous Red Carpet Sauna. Attending, besides the board of the Grand Avenue Business Association, was Chuck McGuire, a veteran city planner. McGuire had been to hundreds of neighborhood meetings in his career. He believed in good planning and did not think special interest groups deserved to benefit at the expense of their fellow citizens. Although he was aware of the association's concerns, he also knew that he had been able to convince nearly everyone else in the city that the new rezoning plan was a good idea, and he did not think that the members of the Grand Avenue Business Association would be any different.

When the routine business of the meeting had been concluded and Doc Chopp had brought out his bottles of wine, McGuire brought out his zoning map. He pointed out the differences that existed between the old zoning and present land use patterns and pointed out how his proposed plan would match existing land uses. That was not what the association wanted to hear. They had just learned from the Macalester study that Grand Avenue had a commercial future, and here was a city planner trying to tie the land to how it was presently being used. The board members would have none of it.

First, they reiterated their points. The proposed new zoning was anti-business, and the business people had been responsible for most of the good things that had happened on the street. It did not allow for the expansion of business, and, if business could not expand, it would die. The street worked just fine under the old zoning, so why fix something that was not broken? The plan called for a dramatic reduction in the land zoned for commercial activity, and, within the "B" zon-

Flourishing locally owned and operated service station at the corner of Hamline and Grand. Father and son owners Joe and Chuck Brost call it "Grand-Wheeler II" because the first station they bought is located further west on Grand at Wheeler. (Dave Lanegran photo.)

ing, very few places existed for businesses that drew customers from outside the immediate Grand Avenue neighborhood. This particularly irritated the group because some businesses on the street actually served a very large section of the metro area. In reality, only half of the customers and business activity came from the immediate neighborhood.

Suspecting the worst, the members accused people in the neighborhood of trying to make a museum out of Grand Avenue. Finally, they told Chuck that they had political friends downtown and that they were going to fight it out in the city council. They implied they would organize and line up the Chamber of Commerce and other powerful interest groups against the zoning plan and the planners.

A few weeks later, another meeting was held. Again Doc Chopp was the host. This time two members of the City Council, Bob Sylvester and Dave Hozza , were in attendance. The two men had acquainted themselves with the details of the street, the study, and the plan and came prepared to hammer out an agreement. At that time, Councilman Hozza lived in Crocus Hill, so he knew the issues personally. He was also uniquely prepared to mediate the issues because he had earned a master's degree in regional planning from the University of North Carolina and had worked as a planner for the St. Paul HRA, as acting planning coordinator and as assistant city administrator. His experience and leadership style made a solution possible.

The meeting began, and everyone brought out their maps and charts. They soon reached agreement on several points. For example, all agreed that there was little chance that the large blocks of apartments would be razed for retail development. It was also clear that most of the kinds of businesses the residents considered to be disruptive to the atmosphere of Grand (such as fast food franchises) would not be attracted to the street anyway because no large parcels of land were available. Those fears were put to rest. Then the planners acknowledged that the business community was not out to exploit Grand Avenue but had a genuine interest in the street and neighborhood. After all, the large number of people operating businesses on Grand could not be denied.

Considering the belligerency of the first meeting, this one was a good session. There appeared to be agreement that Grand would be a "mixed-use street," meaning there would be both thriving businesses and pleasant residential areas. The zone for business would be markedly reduced, but there would be an attempt to put all the areas with obvious commercial potential into one of the business zones. Those few businesses that were defined as "general business" were given appropriate B-3 zoning, although most were defined as local and neighborhood businesses. The session was toasted with rhubarb wine, and the planners went back to City Hall believing that everyone was satisfied. But not everyone was.

On June 6, 1975, in a last ditch effort to maximize the development potential of Grand Avenue, a group of businessmen succeeded in having a motion introduced at the city council that would have rezoned all of Grand Avenue from Dale street to Howell, with the exception of the apartment buildings, as B-3, a general business classification. This event precipitated a flurry of telephone calls and hurried meetings with representatives on all sides. The final meeting was held on June 30 with Councilmen Hozza and Sylvester and resulted in a compromise that involved three zoning classifications; multiple family, community business (B-2), and general business (B-3).

All apartments with more than three units were zoned as multiple family (RM-2), which was their current use. The few existing establishments that required B-3 zoning, such as the funeral home and the car dealerships, were grandfathered in under a B-3 classification. All of the rest of the buildings on the street, from Dale to Howell, whether they were shops, single-family houses or duplexes, were all zoned B-2, for community business. The Grand Avenue Business Association had won. The future growth and development of Grand Avenue had been made as certain as anything could be.

This compromise preserved the pure residential area at the western end of the street. It also achieved the residents' goal of preventing the development of a fast food or franchise row as these businesses required a B-3 zoning and, basically, there weren't many parcels of land left that were zoned B-3. The business community was pleased because now there was ample room for expansion of local business into the housing stock, which was zoned B-2. The large car dealerships were in the last years of their productive life, but the zoning of the locations as B-3 kept alive the possibility for them to be reused.

There was just one problem that no one at the time thought much about. The rules for building within the zones were not discussed in detail, and many people did not consider the fact that, in a business zone, a land owner could build from lot line to lot line. That would, of course, reduce the amount of green and open space along the avenue and would drastically change the character of the street.

This defect in B-2 zoning went unrecognized until Peter Denzer added a lean-to addition onto the front of his home and studio at 814 Grand Avenue. Denzer's addition extended the front of the house all the way to the edge of the sidewalk. And it was perfectly legal. B-2 zoning allowed any kind of addition to a house, even additions that extended out to the sidewalk in front, to the alley in back and to the property lines on either side. No one on Grand had constructed that kind of an addition onto a business property in anyone's memory until Denzer did it, and it created a storm of protest.

Leading the protest was Elberta Matters, then editor of the *Grand Gazette*. In the summer of 1975, District 16 had bought the paper from Swardson for $2,000 and hired Elberta at a salary of $300 per month to edit it. The district council expected the paper to be a vehicle for communication among the residents and businesses of District 16. It was that, but it soon became much more.

Elberta had her own ideas about the paper, and the *Grand Gazette* soon became a strong and controversial element on the street. The paper took stands favoring historic preservation, the planting of trees on Grand; it led the effort to get traffic lights at Grand and Victoria, (the city department in charge lacked vision and was going strictly by the numbers in refusing to install lights despite accidents and many near misses), vigorously protested the destruction of the Uptown Theater and chided the Denzers for the tastelessness (in her opinion) of the shop addition to the house.

In the October 1980 issue of the *Grand Gazette*, Elberta, under a headline "HOW COULD THEY," printed two pictures of the Denzer building, a front and side view, and protested the

addition of a lean-to like structure to the front of a perfectly respectable, though admittedly, hum-drum dwelling in the block between Avon and Victoria. The owners have seen fit to add to the front of their house shop space which in the light of their apparent artistic sensibilities (the husband a writer, sculptor, art photographer; the wife a skilled potter) must surely be considered a least a joke in poor taste at the expense of the neighborhood. The new addition fronts directly on the sidewalk with one window and a very ordinary (stock size and design) door on the front.

Elberta went on to write,

The lean-to, for that is what it most resembles, does not blend with the original design of the house. We must take the developers of this new shop sharply to task for committing such an atrocity. If the atrocity had been committed by someone with an untrained eye, it would have been bad enough. Committed by supposedly artistic individuals, it is a serious crime.[2]

140

City officials, though they did not express their concern in as colorful language as Elberta, were also appalled. The addition to the Denzer building, known in city planning circles as "the shed," led to a change in zoning on Grand Avenue.

Besides the concern almost everyone had about the appearance of Grand, arguments over the supply of parking had become more frequent. Both the merchants and the surrounding residents agreed it was time for a new zoning plan. In 1982, several task forces were assembled, and, in the summer of 1983, four reports were issued by the St. Paul Department of Planning and Economic Development. The reports were in response to special studies, called 40-Acre Studies, that had been conducted for the east and west ends of Grand

Two views of the controversial Peter Denzer building that led to the enactment of B-2C zoning. The addition to the house was built out to the street as was the garage on the east side. The picture with the garage (top) is taken from the east, looking west. The photograph with the statuary in front (bottom) was taken from the west, looking east. (Dave Lanegran photos.)

141

Avenue. The first major step forward to come out of the first plan was a new zoning option.

A city planner by the name of Roger Ryan came up with a solution to the B-2 problem. He suggested a never-heard-of-before zoning designation called B-2C. The B-2 houses and duplexes would be changed to a B-2C designation. Businesses could still be moved into the houses, but the houses could not be changed in any significant way on the outside. No more lean-to additions could be built out to the sidewalk. The residential set-back had to be maintained. There could be no building out to the alley in back or up to the property lines.[3]

The second report was the Grand Avenue Parking Plan, which suggested several ways to ease the parking shortage at the busy commercial intersections. Among its provisions was a requirement that off-street parking must be provided, at least for employees. This was the first time in St. Paul that businesses were required to provide off-street parking. A formula was devised to determine if a business was in compliance. A retail store had to provide one parking space for every 300 square feet of selling space. Furniture stores were allowed up to 800 square feet for each parking space. Most businesses were able to find enough space behind their buildings to comply with the parking requirement.

The third report developed recommendations for a Special Sign District Plan and Ordinance. The goal of this plan was to minimize signage clutter, to improve the readability of signs, and to prohibit signs for products that failed

Two houses that have been converted into businesses. The one on the left was constructed under the earlier B-2 zoning, and the one on the right under B-2C zoning. (Dave Lanegran photo.)

to serve any purpose not directly related to the avenue. Sign colors and materials were required to be compatible with the building and its surroundings, with a minimal amount of color and indirect or subdued lighting used. Wall signs were favored that did not extend perpendicularly from store fronts. Gone were the days when shop owners could build their own signs in their basements and get their husbands to help them hang them. The effect of this ordinance was to dramatically sharpen the image of Grand Avenue.

The fourth and final report was the Grand Avenue Design Guidelines and Action Plan (1983). Its goal was to "build the image of Grand Avenue as a special area and to create an atmosphere that is desirable to both residents and customers." The plan's major points were: (1) decorative lighting should be used to highlight the five major commercial areas (No longer would the Jim Wenglers of the street have to resort to subterfuge to get decorative lighting on the parkway); (2) trees were recommended as a vital part of creating a unified design for the entire length of the avenue because they "pedestrianize" the street; (3) improvements should stress unification of features such as lighting, signs, parking and facades; (4) there should be an increase in the shared use of parking lots; and, (5) parking lots directly facing Grand should be screened.

For a time, these plans guided growth on Grand. But by the end of the 1980s the parking situation was again in crisis. Rezoning for parking occurred in 1989, 1991, and 1992 with the last two zoning changes bringing permit parking

A gift shop at 1752 Grand Avenue. The commercial building was built out to the lot line, a practice prohibited under B-2C zoning. (Dave Lanegran photo.)

Two residences converted
into businesses under the
B2-C zoning provision.
(Dave Lanegran photo.)

programs to the residential streets bordering Grand Avenue. Strongly opposed by most of the merchants, the permit parking prohibited parking on the affected residential streets by anyone not holding a permit. Thus customers and employees of the shops could not park on the residential streets and had to compete for space on Grand Avenue or in the parking lots. The parking lot on Grand owned by the House of Hope Presbyterian Church was made available for employee parking and some limited use was made of it, particularly by employees of the businesses east of Victoria Crossing, but it was largely ignored by those who worked at the Victoria Crossing buildings themselves.

In 1995 tentative discussions began on the establishment of a special design district for Grand Avenue, indicating the wide-spread consensus that existed in maintaining the special character of the street.

Notes

1. *The Avenue 1973* (St. Paul, Minnesota, Macalester College, 1973).

2. Matters, *Grand Gazette*, October 1980.

3. Telephone interview by Billie Young with Roger Ryan, June 15, 1995.

15

Women Business Owners

GRAND AVENUE IS A STREET on which women entrepreneurs have made a difference. Women business owners have been a major presence on the street at least since the 1960s. Teasleys, The Basket Shoppe, the Antique Store, the Record Shop, the Lexington Restaurant, and many others operated without anyone really taking note of how many of the businesses were being run by women. Beginning with the example of the Old Mexico Shop in the early 1970s, women business owners began opening businesses on Grand in increasing numbers until Grand Avenue had a percentage of women business owners more than twice the national average. Nationwide women owners average from fifteen to twenty percent of business owners, but on Grand Avenue they were double that number. A survey conducted by Macalester College in 1988 found that women owned eighty-four of the 202 businesses interviewed by the geography students.[1]

Grand reflected the beginning of a national trend not documented until almost a decade later—that American women were starting twice as many businesses as men. A total of 7.7 million women are currently running their own ventures, about one third of all businesses in the United States.[2]

One of the first actions taken by women business owners on Grand Avenue was to put an end to the queen contests. Mary Rice, Carol Howe, Mary Wilson, and Billie Young all objected to the event, which, in the early 1970s

145

was the principal association event of the year. The male business owners had derived great pleasure from putting the contestants' pictures in their store windows and attending a banquet with the young women. Despite their enjoyment of the queen contest, when women business owners objected, the men agreed that the time had come to make a change, and they gave up the project with few (apparent) regrets.

One of the new women business owners, who happened to be on the board of the business association, suggested that the $3,000 previously spent on the queen contest be invested in colorful banners to be hung from the light poles on Grand. The idea was accepted with enthusiasm, and, within a few weeks, an order was placed with a Minneapolis flag manufacturer for approximately fifty red-and-black flags with the words "Grand Avenue" printed across the banner. Northern States Power gave permission for the flags to be hung from light poles beginning at West Seventh Street, continuing up the hill and down Grand Avenue to Fairview. Each flag cost the association forty-eight dollars.

Most of the members of the Grand Avenue Business Association were standing outside their stores, watching as the colorful flags went up. For an hour, the street looked like the midway at the state fair. Then, thieves struck. Literally, before the last flag had been dropped into its holder on the

Opening of the Red Balloon bookstore in November 1989. Standing in the front of the store are owners Michele Poire Cromer and Carol Erdahl. (*Highland Villager* photo.)

light pole at the western end of Grand, flags from the eastern end were being stolen. People put ladders in the back of pickup trucks to reach the flags. Some poles were bent in U shapes by thieves tugging on the fabric of the flags to get them down. The issue of the *Grand Gazette* that announced the putting up of the flags also contained a black bordered box on the front page reporting that the flags were being stolen. Within a week only a few were left. Doc Chopp and a friend drove a truck down the street and took down the last remaining stragglers before they, too, could be taken. No one was ever arrested for stealing the flags, and none were ever found. If the flags made their way into Macalester or St. Thomas dormitory rooms, they were well-hidden.

The women's idea for a replacement for the queen contest was a failure. Though the queen contest did not reappear, neither did the idea of decorative banners on the street. Jane Tiegen, of the Basket Shoppe, organized a sale to help make up some of the money lost in the flag episode, but it was several years before the budget of the Grand Avenue Business Association recovered from the loss.

Despite the flag disaster, Mike Mischke, *Grand Gazette* editor, believes the presence of women owners and managers with their heightened concern for customer service had a profound impact on the success of the street. Resourcefulness, ingenuity and, above all, attention to serving customers became the route to success for many of the women who opened businesses on Grand. Most businesses were owner-operated, and local residents appreciated the presence of the owner, whether she was sweeping out the store, waiting on customers, cooking in the kitchen or just standing in her doorway watching the passing scene on the street.

Linda Quinn, co-owner with her husband, Peter, of Cafe Latte, Häagen-Dazs Ice Cream, and Bread and Chocolate believes women owners have made a major difference on the street. "Women are just better at listening to customers and providing those things people want to buy," she explained. A good relationship with people and sensitivity to the needs of the people of the neighborhood became a paramount factor in the success of the women-owned businesses on Grand.[3]

Cynthia Gerdes, owner of Creative Kidstuff at 1074 Grand agrees. "Women owners have brought a touch of heart and soul to Grand," she says. "Profits are not the only reason we are in business. I would put it about third in line." Gerdes believes Grand Avenue has the right mix between neighborhood shoppers and customers coming in from out-

Creative Kidstuff at 1074 Grand Avenue. (Dave Lanegran photo.)

side the area. "I just love it. I have never been a mall person. Grand Avenue is the antithesis of a mall. It is an honor for me to be doing business on Grand."[4]

Roxanne Freese, who founded the Bibelot Shop in St. Anthony Park in 1966, opened her second store at 1082 Grand Avenue in 1987. She, too, believes woman owners have made a difference in the ambiance and mood of the street. "There is a different enthusiasm with women," she says. "You see it in the way people greet each other and share information." Though the Bibelot draws from a wide trade area, Roxanne defines her shop as a neighborhood store and strives to maintain a friendly atmosphere.[5]

Nancy Fish opened Bywords, her printing business, in the Summit Hill Mall in 1981 with a male partner, Vic Jarocki. Though they were in business together for several years, they disagreed and eventually parted company over the issue of customer service. Nancy wanted to make a greater effort to meet the needs and desires of her customers, and Vic was concerned about the additional labor involved in offering a higher level of service. They resolved the issue when Nancy bought Vic out and carried on the business alone in an expanded location on Grand.[6]

The presence of so many women in business made a difference in the kinds of businesses that existed on the street, in the store fronts, in the services offered, and in the general ambiance. There were more bouquets of flowers and dishes of candy on counters. There were fewer hard-edged

Maureen McKasy and her sister Mary Pat McKasy in Mary Pat's Paperworks store, 1991. (*Highland Villager* photo.)

and more thoughtful enterprises. One was Learn Me, a children's bookstore owned by Shirley Keenan at 642 Grand. The bookstore was one of the first in the country to emphasize books containing non-sexist role models in literature for children. In a few short years Shirley made such an impression on the publishing world that editors would send her manuscripts of children's books in advance of publication for her comments.

Judith Neren Dean, a family nurse practitioner who also runs the Victoria Gallery of original lithographs at 1114 Grand Avenue, has turned her back yard into an Audubon Society certified bird sanctuary. She took Rick Webb, owner of the Lexington Restaurant, to small claims court when he sent an employee out to cut down her grape vines, which provided cover for the birds and bordered (and, Webb thought, encroached on) his parking lot.[7]

The Summit Hill Mall at Grand was, for a time, occupied entirely by women business owners. In addition to the Old Mexico Shop and Bywords Printing, Jane Lichtscheidel ran a shop selling vintage clothing. Jane had purple hair, drove a Harley Davidson tricycle and sometimes came to work on roller skates. Other tenants were Hattie's Antiques, a shop selling decorative plates, Paula Mannillo's clothing shop, Alma Hayes' miniatures store, Mary Beth Timmers' Toll House, Nimble Fingers, a sewing supplies store owned by Carole Gatten, and Mary and Paul Daley's Treadle Yard Goods.

Because the women business owners had children, youngsters were a familiar sight behind the counters after school, unpacking merchandise or helping customers. Mary Rice remembers that there were four owners with children on the block with Thrice. She and her sister, Martha, had children as did Carol Howe of the Leather Indian and Joyce Yamamoto who had a pottery shop and studio across the street. The children would gather at their mothers' stores after school, and, on occasion, Joyce would invite the children into her studio and let them make simple ornaments and small boxes of clay, which she fired for them in her kilns.

Joyce faced a greater challenge to her resourcefulness one morning when a confused deer wandered up from the river and jumped through the plate glass window of her store. Pottery and tables were overturned and broken as the deer struggled to escape. The episode ended when animal control officers with a tranquilizer gun shot the animal with a dart and got it out of the store.

When Pat and Dick Swinney, with Gail Krey, their sole employee, opened Our Gang Hair Designs shop in 1976 at 1041 Grand, they cut and styled hair Monday through Saturday as well as Thursday evenings and were almost worked to death. Gail remembers that she was so tired that she went home and cried every night. After three weeks they brought in Bill Kaltenburg and Germaine Hall to help out, and all five are still there.

The most dramatic solution to childcare for working mothers on Grand was created by Karen Tarrant, a Grand Avenue attorney. Formerly a partner in a downtown law firm, Karen found the demands of being a full-time partner in a law firm and those of being a good mother almost impossible to reconcile. "It came down to an either/or option," she recalled. "Either you risk the developing relationship with your baby . . . or you sacrifice your career." No matter how swamped with work she was, "I had to drop everything at 4:30 and go home, so the baby sitter could catch her bus."

When Karen, in the middle of preparations for a major law suit, got a call at work from her sitter telling her that her son Ben had pulled a stereo down and smashed a finger, she knew she had to make changes in how she worked. Her solution was to borrow heavily to purchase the

Attorney Karen Tarrant with sons Patrick and Ben in front of her professional building at 1539 Grand Avenue. (Photo by Wayne Thompson.)

three-story seventy-two-year-old house at 1539 Grand Avenue and convert it into professional offices with childcare facilities on site. The building had been a rooming house for Macalester college students and required extensive remodeling. Karen converted it into eight offices with a conference room and on-site secretarial and word-processing services. Crucial to the success of the venture were the two rooms at the back equipped and staffed as a licensed day-care center. In October 1984, Karen and other professional women took over the offices, and several children, including Karen's son, Ben, moved into the day-care center. The working women in Karen's Rowan Professional Building on Grand had found a way to continue their careers and their relationships with their children at the same time.[8]

When Jim and Mary Ann Kowalski bought the Red Owl grocery store at the corner of Grand and Syndicate in 1983, the store was dying. Jim, who had been a district manager of another grocery business, looked at the surrounding neighborhood and thought there was no reason why the store could not survive. But to do so it would have to relate better to the local residents. He and Mary Ann invested their life savings and their daughter Chris' college money in the business and, the day the deal was closed, brought in members of their family to help run the store.

Chris took over one of the cash registers and talked her classmates at Derham Hall high school to hire on to run the other registers. Tom's father stocked and kept the pop machines filled. His mother and Mary Ann counted the money. His sister Deb and her husband came from California, she to manage the store and he to work in it. On the night of the Derham Hall graduation, they almost had to close the store. Most of the young women cashiers had the night off to attend their graduation.

Deb credits the store's success to the presence of family members (fourteen currently work in the store) and to their having gained the confidence of the neighborhood. When a power outage threatened the contents of the freezers in the neighborhood, Kowalski's, which had power, put a sign in the window saying they would take packages of frozen food from residents and keep it cold in their freezers until the power came back on.

Four days a week, buses bring in senior citizens from eleven different high rises to do their shopping, and Kowalski's has free coffee and cookies waiting. Carry-out staff are instructed to help elderly or handicapped shoppers by carrying groceries up stairs and into kitchens if necessary.

In the winter, the store staff jump-starts cars and pushes vehicles out of snow drafts in the parking lot.

Deb's favorite day of the year to work in the store is Christmas Eve. Their first Christmas Eve, they had planned to close at 4:00 P.M., but customers kept coming. They sent most of the staff home, and the family ran the store—staying open several hours past their intended closing time. Later they learned that the union was unhappy with them for having stayed open, so now they close at 4:00 P.M. But the family members still work the store that day. As Deb says, "We see our friends; everyone is rushing around, happy, filled with holiday spirit." When Jim and Mary Ann bought the store, it was grossing about $50,000 per week. Twelve years later the store grosses around $350,000 weekly.[9]

One of the great success stories for a woman-run business, not just of Grand Avenue but of the region, is that of Bread and Chocolate, and Cafe Latte. Linda and Peter Quinn were among the young urban pioneers who moved into the Ramsey Hill neighborhood in 1975. They bought the house at 691 Portland for $18,000 from the Wilder Foun-

Cafe Latte, 1988. (*Highland Villager* photo.)

152

dation, which had used the building for offices. Linda was a medical technician at Midway Hospital and Peter a salesman selling Jenny Lee macaroni products to grocery stores.

The historic renovation going on in the neighborhood captured their imagination, and they soon became involved in Old Town Restorations and in buying old or burned-out houses for a few thousand dollars and restoring them. Linda insisted on authentic restoration and did the decorating herself, finding authentic period doorknobs and fireplace mantles. When interest rates soared in the early 1980s, they left the building restoration business and looked for something else to do in the neighborhood. Peter's company wanted to transfer him to another city, but the Quinns did not want to leave St. Paul. Linda was pregnant at the time and loved Häagen-Dazs ice cream, which was dispensed from a small window at the side of the Garuda Restaurant in Victoria Crossing West. They investigated opening an ice cream store on Grand Avenue, and, when Häagen-Dazs offered them the franchise, they took it.

Besides being a medical technician, Linda was also a cook with a drawerful of family recipes for healthful breads and soups. Next door to the Häagen-Dazs ice cream store in Victoria Crossing, they opened Bread and Chocolate, a shop selling baked goods and beverages, with a small space devoted to sandwiches and soups for lunch patrons. The shop did well, but Linda wanted a location where she could carry a counter full of wholesome and nutritious soups and salads.

When Howard Bergerud purchased the opera building on the southeast corner of Grand and Victoria to convert into Victoria Crossing South, Peter and Linda signed a lease on a space on the street they called Cafe Latte. Their idea was to offer wholesome breads, soups, and salads, principally for take out. The Quinns did no market study before opening their business. As Linda says, "If we had done a market study, I would have chickened out. We just wanted to serve the kinds of foods we liked to eat."[10]

It turned out that the kinds of foods the Quinns liked to eat were what the market wanted on Grand Avenue. They ground their own whole wheat for bread (it makes a moister loaf, according to Linda), used Linda's family recipes for the soups and salads they served, installed the first espresso coffee machine in St. Paul and prohibited smoking. Within a few weeks, they discovered that what their customers wanted was not take out, as they had thought, but a place to sit down and eat Linda's food. They closed for remodeling and reopened as one of the most popular eateries in the Twin

Cities. Lines extend out the door until late at night, and the restaurant's gross per square foot is one of the highest in the upper midwest.

Diners at Cafe Latte see Peter Quinn "out front" supervising the dining room and serving staff and assume that he is the force behind the success of the enterprise. They are mistaken. It is Linda who runs the production, devises the recipes, determines the menus, invents new kinds of breads (apricot currant cashew, Finnish farmer's rye, orange ricotta, jalapeno cheddar, Sicilian picnic) and supervises the kitchen and baking staff.

The customer base for Cafe Latte is broad. As might be expected, there are the young professionals to whose tastes the Quinns inadvertently but accurately appealed. But younger people, the fast-food crowd, also come to the restaurant for a break from hamburgers. And for elderly patrons, Linda makes hundreds of egg salad sandwiches. The restaurant now draws tours from the Mall of America. In Linda's opinion, "If people are going to go someplace in St. Paul, it will be to Grand Avenue."

Although each woman entrepreneur has her own very personal story, some broad generalizations can be made about the group. Most of the business women, eighty-seven percent, were related to an entrepreneur. This figure is significantly higher than the national average of seventy-five percent and indicates that the women came from a culture that respected and encouraged business life and a certain amount of independence.

According to national statistics, half of all female entrepreneurs in the 1980s started their careers after a major turning point in their lives. Most frequent causes were the loss of a job or a divorce. Yet on Grand Avenue, only one-third of the women entered business under such circumstances. On Grand, women were not entering business under duress. A great many of them also came from the area around the avenue.[11]

The large number of women entrepreneurs on Grand may be the result of two significant factors. First, women feel safe in their places of business. While there were shoplifters and the occasional purse snatcher, after the late 1970s the avenue did not have incidents of armed robbery or violent crime. Second, there were a set of early role models who were very visible and highly successful. Billie Young, Mary Wilson, Carole Howe, Michelle Poire Odegard, the women of Paperback Traders and others were the objects of numerous feature stories in the newspapers. Women trying to decide whether or not to go into business consulted with them as they made their decisions.

The success of the business women on Grand struck a chord among women who could envision themselves running some sort of a business. The established businesswomen provided a support group for newcomers and helped out in a variety of ways. Once the number of women engaged in business began to expand, it became easier for other women to make the decision to start a business, and a special atmosphere on Grand was created. Each new enterprise encouraged another to join until a little boom occurred. By the mid 1990s an equilibrium was established, but the number of women in business on Grand continued to increase, propelled, in part, by past relationships. Robin Brandt opened Minnesota Seasons in Victoria Crossing West. Martha Gaarder opened her business, Woodlines, at 1326 Grand Avenue in October 1995. Though she was a biology and religion major in college, Gaarder's true love was furniture making. She learned how to lay ceramic tiles from Billie Young, of the Old Mexico Shop, and later made bookcases for a national furniture distributor. This led to the opening of two retail stores—one of which was on Grand Avenue. Business women throughout the metropolitan area, whether they are attorneys, veterinarians, woodworkers, or cooks, list Grand Avenue as their first choice of a location for opening or expanding a business.

Notes

1. *The Avenue 1988*, (St. Paul, Minnesota, Macalester College, 1988).

2. Laura Pedersen, "Minding Your Business," *New York Times*, July 30, 1995.

3. Interview by Billie Young with Linda and Peter Quinn, August 29, 1995.

4. Interview by Billie Young with Cynthia Gerdes, September 15, 1995.

5. Interview By Billie Young with Roxanne Freese, September 15, 1995.

6. Nancy Fish.

7. Interview by Billie Young with Judith Neren, September 1995.

8. Interview by Billie Young with Karen Tarrant, August 1995.

9. Interview by Billie Young with Deb Kowalski, July 18, 1995.

10. Peter and Linda Quinn.

11. *The Avenue 1987*, (St. Paul, Minnesota, Macalester College, 1987), pp. 63-66.

Zachmann, the Grand Avenue Florist placed this advertisement in the *Dual City Blue Book of 1913-1914.* The shop was located where Kowalski's market now stands. (Ad courtesy of Judith Neren Dean of Victoria Gallery. Photo by Laura Church.)

Albert Zachmann

WHOLESALE and RETAIL

Grand Avenue
FLORIST

Cut Flowers in Season

Tel. N. W. Midway 943   Tel. Tri-State 7726

1247 Grand Avenue   ST. PAUL, MINN.

The three generations of the Thomas family who have owned the Thomas pharmacy. Founder Clarence Thomas is in the portrait above the door with son Michael and grandson Jim below. The business opened as the Rosedale Pharmacy in 1922. (Laura Church photo.)

16

A Business Community Develops

THE STORY OF GRAND AVENUE is a story of people's life experiences, the decisions they made, their responses to crisis. The street is the sum of all of the people who have lived their social and economic lives on and around it. People are the engines of history. Grand's history is that of the day-by-day actions of a variety of people who chose this urban street on which to act out their life stories. If there is a constant, that constant is change. Like a barometer registering the changing pressure of the air, Grand Avenue has for 100 years reflected the changes in the economy and the shifts in philosophy and life style of a major portion of the city's population. From the electric car to the self-service grocery store to the coffee house, Grand Avenue has been the place for experimentation and the setting of trends.

The genius of Grand Avenue, however, may be that, while adapting to and leading change, the street has also supported businesses of amazing longevity. The Grand Avenue Hardware store, a mainstay of the neighborhood, was founded by Elbert Smolik in 1917, and his granddaughter, Nancy, is still employed there. The store passed from Elbert to his son, Don Smolik, who sold it to his employees in 1994 in an ESOP arrangement. The two principal owners now are Jim and Jeannine Solin. Jeannine went to work in the store in 1962 and never left. Her husband, Jim, joined the staff in 1976.

In the Grand Avenue tradition of extraordinary service, the store, from its founding until the mid 1970s, wrapped and held Christmas presents for its customers, delivering them to neighborhood homes on Christmas Eve. Jim still takes his tools to the homes of elderly residents to install phone jacks. The store provides free delivery even on the occasions when the quavering voice of an elderly customer calls and says, "I need a measuring cup right now."

The second floor of the hardware store housed the Andahazy Ballet, a dance school that was in the same location for forty-seven years. Founded by Larond Andahazy, a teacher from Russia, and continued by his son, Marius, the school taught classical ballet to generations of aspiring dancers, sounding on Saturday mornings "like a herd of elephants" to Jim Solin in the hardware store below.[1]

The Thomas Liquor store at 2047 Grand Avenue has been in business since 1922. When it opened, it was known as Rosedale Pharmacy, named after the surrounding neighborhood known then as Rosedale Park. Highland Park had not yet been developed, and the location was on the outskirts of St. Paul in an outlying and largely undeveloped community. In the late 1920s, pharmacist Clarence J. Thomas purchased the business and changed the name of the pharmacy to Thomas Pharmacy. The business has been owned by the Thomas family ever since.

Clarence Thomas was known for the gin he made for his personal use and for gifts to friends, but his son says the pharmacy did not sell liquor until after Prohibition was repealed, when a liquor department was added to the store. The business became a full-service liquor store in the 1950s, and the name was changed from Thomas Pharmacy to Thomas Liquors. Current owners are Jim and Michael Thomas, the son and grandson of Clarence.[2]

The Grandendale Pharmacy, located at the corner of Grand Avenue and Dale Streets, has been in that location at least since 1925, according to Jim Miller, who owned the business for twenty-two years.

Paul Rudolph lived at Milton and St. Clair and, as a boy in 1953, hung around the Pure Oil gas station on the corner of Grand and Oxford. At that time, five gas stations crowded one block on Grand between Oxford and Lexington. Paul made himself useful, and, in 1954, the owner, Vincent F. Straus, hired the boy to pump gas and clean up around the pits in the repair bays. One thing led to another, and, in 1976, Paul Rudolph bought the station and has been there ever since. His three sons, David, John, and Dan work there with their father, pumping gas from the two pumps and repairing cars. The pits are gone, replaced by hydraulic lifts,

but the old gas station architecture of the 1920s remains—
the steep-pitched roof, the tiny twelve-by-fifteen-foot office,
and the old trees shading the station from the street.[3]

Don LaValle's story mirrors that of Paul Rudolph's.
He, too, as a boy growing up at the corner of Summit and
Avon, hung around Lloyd's Texaco station at 985 Grand. In
1949, as a sophomore in high school, he started working at
the station, washing cars and pumping gas. By 1951, he was
working full time at the station, and, in 1954, he became a
partner with the owner Howard Lloyd.

The rise to ownership was not easy. According to
LaValle, he was a wild youth who recklessly spent his pay-
checks on cars and girl friends, came to work late, often let
himself into the gas station at four o'clock in the morning to
sleep off too many drinks and had to be awakened and
sobered up by Lloyd when he came in to work in the morning. Looking back, Don says he "doesn't know how he tolerated me." But Lloyd saw something in the reckless Don and
began withholding a quarter of his paycheck, putting it in the
bank for him and forcing him to save. That was the money
Don later used as a partial down payment for his half of the
service station.

Don credits Lloyd for "forming my outlook on life, my
personality, by the things he did. He was like a father to me."
The kinds of "things he did" were to service the car of a
neighborhood woman having financial problems and never
send her a bill. Lloyd made quiet gifts of money to people in
trouble without any expectation of being paid back. Don says
that up to half of their car repair business was done on credit, sealed not with a credit card, but a handshake. Customers
were people from the neighborhood, where Don himself lived
at 952 Goodrich.

Lloyd's Automotive Service
at 985 Grand Avenue.
(Dave Lanegran photo.)

In 1975, Don bought the other half of the partnership in the station from Lloyd and ran it until 1990 when he sold out to Dan Burns. LaValle still hangs around the station, as he did as a teenager, helping solve the more difficult problems with the cars and calling customers to make certain they are happy with the service they have received. He still remembers people by the cars they drive. Wendell Fritz, when he first came around helping organize the Grand Avenue Business Association, drove a 1963 white Plymouth. Dr. George Young, Superintendent of Schools, drove a beige Volkswagon. He recalls the day the owners of the Old Mexico Shop brought their green Dodge van in to be serviced, and the interior of the car had a disagreeable odor. It turned out to be the lingering smell from some insufficiently cured shark's jaws they had hauled home from Mexico.

It is significant to LaValle that many of the Grand Avenue business owners he knew lived in the neighborhood: George Burns, John McGowan, Fran O'Connell, George Margolis. "I had a good life on Grand Avenue," he says. "I enjoyed cars, people, business. It was a very rewarding thing."[4]

Abbott Paint at 1808 Grand was started by Howard "Mike" Abbott, Jr., in 1945. He still runs the store with help from his three sons, Kevin, David, and Stephen. The boys worked in the store as children, dusting, stocking shelves, driving the delivery truck. Kevin estimates that they recognize more than seventy-five percent of their customers and can call most of them by name. He credits their emphasis on service for the store's success.

Employees, too, tend to stay at their jobs on Grand. While Don Ryan of the Lexington Restaurant may hold the record at fifty-one years, Margaret Ann Francis has been working at the Grandendale Drug store for thirteen years and

Charlemagne Jewelry Store at 1262 Grand Avenue, showing the building in 1990 before (left) and in June 1995 after renovation (right). (Photos courtesy of Charles and Harriet Fogarty.)

now waits on the children of children she used to chase around the candy aisle. Pharmacist James LaVahn has been at Grandendale for fourteen years.

The oldest jewelry store on Grand is Charlemagne, which was originally opened in 1974 in a house at 2081 Grand. The owners, jewelry designers Charles W. Fogarty and his wife, Harriet K., two years later moved the shop to a store front location at 1276 Grand, mainly because the store, formerly Rotter's Furrier, had a walk-in safe.

Despite the presence of the safe, Charlemagne had a robbery that was foiled by the extraordinary actions of an employee, Nori Nonaka. On a morning in 1984, Nonaka was showing a tray of rings to three men, when they suddenly grabbed the tray from his hands and fled the store. The men jumped into a waiting car and would have gotten away had not Nonaka run after them and dived head first through the open window on the driver's side of the car. Nonaka grabbed the car keys, turned off the ignition and confiscated the keys. The moving car veered off the street onto the parkway and stopped. The three thieves fled, but not before Nonaka had torn the shirt off one of them. The men left behind most of the jewelry, their jackets, billfolds with their identification, and the car.

In 1989, the Fogartys purchased the Zackman house at 1262 Grand Avenue. The house had been built in 1889. The Fogartys spent two years converting the house into the present Charlemagne Jewelry store, one of the most successful house conversions on the avenue. The building is on five levels and houses their design and manufacturing studios as well as the retail store. Both Harriet and Charles have been named two of the one hundred best jewelry designers in North America by the American Gem Trade Association.[5]

Bill Skally bought the apartment building at 620-624 Grand Avenue in 1975 and opened his tax service in one of the basement apartments. At first, customers were fearful of coming to the intersection of Grand and Dale, and employees had to be walked to their cars at night. But as the reputation of Grand improved, so did Skally's tax business. Now his business consists of sixty percent out-of-state clients and the rest neighbors and customers living within five miles of Grand Avenue. Skally served on the board of the Grand Avenue Business Association beginning in 1989 and was president in 1993 and 1994.

Bill Muska was serving in the Army in World War II when he loaned his father $500 to purchase a piece of property at 700 Grand Avenue from the Johnson Sheet Metal

Company. The elder Muska, an immigrant from Czechoslovakia, had a small electrical contracting business, and the space he bought for it on Grand was a small one, about twenty by thirty feet without a basement. When Bill returned from service, he joined his father in the business, eventually remodeling and expanding the shop into the retail Muska Lighting Center. "My father had always dreamed of having a shop on Grand Avenue close to Crocus Hill where many of his best customers were located," Bill remembered.[6]

In 1916, a baker by the name of Reino Wuollet went to work for the Federal Bakeshop at the corner of Lake and Hennepin in Minneapolis. He was still there in 1926 when a high school student named Martin Olson got a part-time job washing pans and cleaning up around the bakery. The two men became friends, and, within a few years, both had become managers of Federal Bakeshops—Reino in Austin and Marty in Duluth. By 1944, Reino was ready to establish his own shop and bought a bakery at Fiftieth and Penn in Minneapolis. At about the same time, Marty opened his Bungalow Bakery in downtown St. Paul. After service in World War II, Marty returned to St. Paul and moved his bakery from downtown to 1080 Grand Avenue. Through the years, the two bakers remained close friends, and, when Marty decided to retire in 1977, he sold his Bungalow Bakery to Reino. When Reino retired, his three sons: Jim, Ben, and Dan took over his bakery business. And when Marty Olson died, one of the pallbearers was Jim Wuollet, the son of Marty's old friend Reino.

Customers who line up for service at Wuollet's Bungalow Bakery counter are buying baked goods from an establishment that has been in operation, under one man-

Muska Lighting at 700 Grand Avenue. (Dave Lanegran photo.)

162

agement or another, for more than half a century.[7]

Most people who come to the avenue are there to shop, visit with friends in a coffee house, or have dinner in one of the restaurants. But there are other reasons for coming to Grand that are not immediately apparent to the casual visitor. On the east end of Grand, just before the street turns to go down the hill toward Fort Road, stand three houses, connected by walkways and set back from the street at the top of high banks. The houses are painted dark colors

Children looking in Wuollet's Bungalow bakery shop window at 1088 Grand Avenue. (*Highland Villager* photo.)

and, except for the fact they are well maintained, they look almost unoccupied. Most visitors drive up Grand Avenue without ever noticing the three connected houses.

But for others, the three houses are a destination and a life line. They are the first shelters for battered women ever built in the United States. In October 1974 Women's Advocates opened its first shelter at 584 Grand Avenue. The Grand Avenue Business Association welcomed the newcomers to the street and contributed money. From that beginning, in a single house, the shelter has grown to encompass three substantial houses, all connected by protected walkways. Forty-five women and children are in residence in the houses at any given time. While the average stay is fifteen days, some come for periods as short as a night, while others stay for as long as sixty days. Since that opening in 1974, more than 18,000 women and children have found shelter in the three houses on Grand. Every year almost 500 women and from 700 to 800 children are admitted. A staff of twenty-five, led by the director Lisbet Wolf provide counseling, housing, and legal services. According to Wolf, nine out of ten applicants for admission to the houses are turned away. But "if the woman is battered and we have space," Wolf says, she will be taken in.[8]

A special relationship exists between Macalester College and Grand Avenue. Although the small liberal arts college prides itself on its traditions of academic excellence and internationalism, it is one of a handful of nationally recognized liberal arts colleges located in the middle of a city. This wonderful location affords its students and faculty the opportunity to go in and out of their "Ivory Tower" with ease. Many members of the college community use this location to follow the admonition to "think globally and act locally." Thus, while Macalester is a unique Grand Avenue institution, in many ways it is analogous to a business. It has a payroll, pays assessments and uses city services. For many years, the college was represented on the board of the Grand Avenue Business Association. It is, however, also a residential community, and its campus is a park with a sizable sports facility. It both generates traffic and provides green space. Graduation ceremonies, replete with bagpipes and parades of faculty and students in medieval academic dress, are held on the main college green adjacent to Grand Avenue and in full view of passing traffic. Faculty and students of the geography and urban studies departments have used Grand Avenue as one of their laboratories for twenty-five years. St. Thomas University dominates the western-most blocks of Grand

Avenue but has not been involved with development of the street to the degree that Macalester College has.

Ever since the trustees of Macalester College paid a bonus to the street railroad company to electrify their service and gave the company a right of way through the campus, Grand Avenue and the college have been inextricably linked. For most of the modern period, the college has tried to ignore the street. Students constantly jaywalk across it. Each student must cross Grand Avenue a minimum of 1,500 times during his years at Macalester. Fortunately, no one has been killed by a car, although there have been a few broken bones and severe bruises over the years. Until the mid-1960s, students and others parked cars on the portion of Grand that runs through the campus. When the Weyerhaeuser chapel was built on the mall just south of Grand, the architects tried to give the campus a strong landscape symbol that would be seen by motorists on the street. At the same time, parking along the street was eliminated. This made crossing safer for the jaywalkers and gave passing motorists views of the green campus and red brick buildings.

Several dormitories were built north of Grand Avenue during the campus enrollment boom of the mid-1960s. This resulted in dormitory complexes on both sides of Grand. The divisions of students into two residential areas

The renovated Old Main and Wallace Library are visible from Grand Avenue on the south side of the main campus green. (Sketch courtesy of Alexander Hill, Macalester College. Photo by Laura Church.)

abetted the development of the tradition of the Grand Snowball Fight. When weather conditions are perfect (a fresh fall of several inches of sticky snow and a mild temperature) a spontaneous snow ball fight of Armageddon proportions will break out between students from the rival dormitory complexes. During the frenzy of the battle, passing cars are bombarded and woe to any macho motorists who stop to challenge the throwers. After the students have achieved a de facto closing of the street, the police arrive and park their cars crosswise on Grand at each side of the campus to de jure close the street and save the motorists from the snow barrage. Throwing snow soon grows boring, and the students retreat to the comfort of their dormitories, once again giving the street back to traffic.

The Campus Plan of 1968 tried to undo Macalester's historic relationship with Grand Avenue once and for all. A Texas-based planning firm advocated closing Grand entirely and replacing the commercial buildings west of the campus with a large multipurpose structure that would include some of the existing businesses as well as college functions. The men behind this plan were totally out of touch with the community. The unfortunate vice president charged with the task of unveiling the plan at the community meeting was vilified and hooted off the stage. Needless to say, the plan was never implemented.

In the spring of 1971, students took over Grand Avenue as part of their protest against the invasion of Cambodia by the United States Armed Forces. That unhappy time was epitomized by the frustrated students stopping equally frustrated commuters and trying to persuade them to join the anti-war movement. Fortunately, the students were not able to build a barricade, and no one was hurt before the police restored order. The college dismissed students early that spring. Relationships between the campus and the neighborhood had reached their nadir.

Although the college administration was slow to formally abandon the Grand Plan, it spent the remainder of the 1970s trying to mend relations with the neighborhood. In 1982, Lanegran was hired as the executive director of a special college fund, High Winds Fund, established by Dwight Wallace, founder of *Readers' Digest* and primary benefactor of Macalester. The fund was to be used by the college to protect the beauty, serenity, and security of the campus neighborhood. In addition to restoring and rebuilding dozens of houses in the early 1980s, a plan was launched that would have redeveloped the north side of Grand between

Macalester Street and Cambridge Avenue. The design called for a mixed residential and commercial block with a parking ramp. After investing several thousand dollars in plans and options, the administration determined that more planning was needed before an expansion could be undertaken.

In 1987, the college collaborated with the Planning and Economic Development Department of the City of St. Paul and the local businesses in a Neighborhood Partnership Program designed to beautify Grand. Macalester contributed $153,357 to narrow Grand Avenue where it went through the campus, bury power lines, install decorative lights and plant trees. This money was matched by the city program and local property owners and decorative lighting was installed on the commercial blocks west of the campus.

For the students, Grand Avenue is part of the social space. They shop in the stores, eat in the restaurants, frequent the movies and hang out in the coffee shops. Here most students come in contact with other residents of the city. Even though Grand sunders the campus, it also is the seam that ties the students to the greater community around them. The students whole-heartedly support the vision of Grand as a diverse landscape that encourages a lively social life. For them, the central college green blends effortlessly into the bustling shopping street.

In 1931, a date within the memories of some living residents, most of the businesses on Grand were tiny operations, run out of people's houses and apartments. Doctors, nurses, dentists, music teachers, tailors, and librarians operated small independent businesses in their apartments. Each block had at least one grocer or butcher. The shops delivered orders in the area every day except Sunday; some even had two deliveries daily. The Piggly Wigglys were the first stores to experiment with self-service, and Grand Avenue boasted three of the new super stores. Few restaurants or clothing stores, however, could be found on the street in the 1930s.

The catastrophe of the Depression during the 1930s was reflected on Grand, and many businesses closed. Then, following World War II, business picked up again, and, by 1955, the street had attained ninety-two percent of the 1931 figure. Just when the street appeared to be well on the way to recovery, conditions worsened, and, by 1978, the number of businesses had fallen to 235 or eighty-seven percent of the 1931 level.

Besides the numbers of businesses, there was a change in the kinds of businesses that operated on the street.

From 1931 to 1988, there was a marked decline in neighborhood-oriented establishments and a steady increase in businesses that served a larger area—such as plumbing establishments and wholesalers of auto parts. While the number of neighborhood-based establishments fell thirty-three percent from 120 to forty, the number of metro-oriented businesses quadrupled, growing from twenty to eighty. The number of both gas stations and grocery stores peaked in 1931. By the 1980s the number of grocery stores had declined to ten percent of the peak year, while gas stations survived a little better, falling to forty percent of the 1931 level.[9]

After falling in the 1970s, the number of businesses began to increase again in the late 1980s, due principally to the conversion of the car dealerships to mini malls. The development of Victoria Crossing by Jim Wengler and his associates brought about a dramatic change in the business climate. Wengler and other new business owners created a new Grand Avenue. The frumpy, decaying neighborhood shopping and apartment strip began to perk up. In just two years, the number of businesses jumped from 235 to 246, a five-percent increase.

An intersection-by-intersection examination of the number of businesses illustrates the influence of the malls in bringing commercial activity to the street. The business community centered on Victoria Street had been dominated by car dealerships and a half-filled office block in 1961 with a total of twenty-seven businesses in the area. By 1978, the number had inched up to thirty. By 1988, the post-mall era, the number had exploded to forty-one, and, in 1995, there were fifty-four businesses at the intersection, exactly double the 1961 level.[10]

The Grand-Lexington intersection has been more stable. After a slight increase in 1988, the number of businesses fell back to the 1961 level, a reflection of the fact that the blocks were built up early, and existing businesses have expanded to take up the space of smaller shops that moved. Slightly further west of Lexington, the availability of houses in the B-2C zone attracted a large number of businesses, while the intersections further west at Grand and Cambridge and Grand and Fairview, that had no malls, remained essentially unchanged during the thirty-five-year period.

At the Oxford intersection, the static Summit Hill Mall was redesigned. Originally built as a storage facility for a moving company's vans and later as a roller skating rink, the building had vast areas of underutilized space. A 1.2 million dollar renovation took off the front corner of the building to make room for a fifteen-space parking lot and gave each retail shop a window onto Grand. The new design was supported by the city planning staff and the Grand Avenue Business Association but ran into resistance from the Summit Hill Association. The guidelines of that association were opposed to parking lots in the front of buildings, as it raised the specter of the suburban franchise row. The dispute was eventually resolved, the building completed, and the intersection had a net gain of three businesses.

By 1988, there were seven mini malls on Grand: the Mac Market, Crocus Common, Victoria Crossing West, Victoria Crossing East, Victoria Cross South, Milton Mall, and Oxford Mall. Although the malls were scattered from Macalester Street to Grotto, four were located within a one-block area near Victoria.

Not all the malls were equally successful. The Summit Hill Mall was in the doldrums until its renovation. The White Lily restaurant gave Crocus Common a good

The Oxford Mall at Grand and Oxford. A corner was cut out of the existing building to make space for the parking lot and to give each business a window onto the street. (Dave Lanegran photo.)

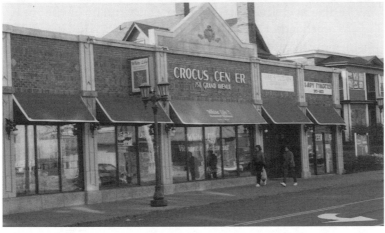

Crocus Center, formerly Crocus Common. This was the third mall to be built in a converted automobile showroom on Grand. (Dave Lanegran photo.)

The Mac Market Mall next to the Macalester College campus was converted from an auto body shop to a mini mall by Macalester College. It contains the Table of Contents restaurant and the Hungry Mind Book Store. The Hungry Mind, owned by David Unowsky, is one of the nation's leading independent bookstores. The oldest bookstore on Grand, it is the publisher of the Hungry Mind Review and has a book publishing division. The Hungry Mind also sponsors an extensive series of readings and public appearances by authors in collaboration with Macalester College. The store is an innovator in the business community of Grand Avenue. (Dave Lanegran photo.)

anchor, but a large amount of interior space was not visible from the street, making it difficult to rent, and a portion of it remained empty.

While the Mac Market was full and appeared to be quite stable, the college administration had further plans for the structure. The book store expanded into a pet food store space, and the Phoenix Vietnamese restaurant was replaced with the Table of Contents. This changed the nature of the mall, making it more attractive to a broader clientele.

The Victoria Crossing malls were uniformly successful for most of the tenants (if not always for the owners) and rents zoomed to match the new image. In 1980, rent in Victoria Crossing East cost four dollars per square foot. Eight years later, this had climbed to twenty-five dollars per square foot with common area costs bringing total rent to thirty-five dollars or more per square foot. This was higher than the rent in many downtown locations and in other retail areas in the Twin Cities. By 1988, the commercial pattern was dominated by retailing (47.5%) and services (39%). Restaurants were on the rise and accounted for thirteen percent of the total.

Altogether, between 1980 and 1988, the number of businesses increased 13.5 percent from 245 to 283. The business climate was wonderful. Not only were there more businesses, they were larger than at any time since the car dealerships had vacated the street. One type of business grew more than any other, however, and that was restaurants.

The growth in restaurants was phenomenal. In 1976, only fifteen eating places could be found on Grand. By 1988, there were thirty-five. A whopping sixty-eight percent of the restaurants were less than five years old. In large measure, that was the result of national trends. In that same period,

The Uptowner Restaurant on the southwest corner of Grand and Lexington. (Dave Lanegran photo.)

the food services share of the consumer's food dollar increased from thirty-three percent in 1970 to forty-one percent in 1980. In addition, restaurant sales increased 3.2% between 1984 and 1986. Americans were choosing to eat out more frequently than at any time previously.

The reason so many Twin Cities diners were coming to Grand was the conversion of the street from a convenience shopping strip to social space. Diners in search of a total experience could find interesting menus served in tastefully rebuilt old structures, and Grand Avenue had the resources needed to create a special ambiance. The mix of apartments, houses, and businesses created a comfortable and safe neighborhood feeling. Its accessibility to the Rice Park cultural district made it a popular place for pre-theater dinner or after-concert refreshments.

The restaurants on Grand offer fare for every price range or taste and can be divided into five broad categories: casual-family, traditional, contemporary, fast-food, and retail restaurants. There are ethnic or geographically specialized cuisines found in each category. The most numerous group are the casual-family restaurants with sixteen establishments, half of which are obviously ethnic (Mexican, Hebrew Kosher, Greek, Vietnamese, Lebanese). These restaurants offer full service but are informal, serving sandwiches, pizza, and inexpensive dinner specials.

The ethnic restaurants are relatively new to Grand. Generally small and owner operated, they serve a menu based on the cuisine of their owners' homeland. They have, however, gradually Americanized their menus and service. Almost all involve the labor of large numbers of family members.

The Vietnamese restaurants give the street a somewhat exotic flare. The new cuisine is popular with young people. More flavorful than the Cantonese food that dominated the menus of Chinese restaurants and more interesting than the ubiquitous pizza, these friendly inexpensive restaurants have become the hang-outs of college students and the young families in the neighborhood.

The Acropol Restaurant fits the description of ethnic restaurants in some ways but not in others. The Acropol is not a newcomer to Grand, and it succeeded when it abandoned its attempts to serve what the owners thought was American food, and turned instead to Greek cuisine. The Acropol was opened in 1975 by Aris and Cassandra Apostolou who had emigrated from Greece in 1956 with their year-old infant Christina. They had come to Minneapolis because Cassandra had an aunt there, who also owned a restaurant. The Apostolous began their careers in food service busing dishes, Aris at night and Cassandra during the day so that one of them could be at home to take care of the baby. Cassandra remembers difficult times when Aris was ill and could not work, and she literally had no food in the house. A neighbor gave them a chicken, which she boiled three times to make ever-weaker soup for her family.

The restaurant they purchased on Grand was Martin's, a mom-and-pop cafe serving roast beef sandwiches and peas to a largely elderly clientele. Aris continued with the same menu and found that, while Martin's had succeeded serving home-style American food, the Apostolous could

Grand Avenue near the Acropol restaurant and Paperback Trader. (*Highland Villager* photo.)

not. Fewer and fewer customers came to the restaurant. Though they were open every day from 6:00 A. M. until 10:00 P.M. at night, they were rapidly losing the life savings they had invested in their business. Cassandra remembers that after cleaning up the kitchen at midnight they would sit in their empty restaurant and ask themselves what they were doing wrong. After six months of almost no business, Aris changed his menu. Gone were the roast beef sandwiches. In their place he served what he knew best how to make, Greek gyros sandwiches.

Slowly customers began to come for the Greek food. The turning point came when Cassandra opened their door one morning at 6:00 A.M. and found a note stuck in the jamb from Steve and Sharon, hosts of the Channel 5 television program "Twin Cities Today." The note complimented them on their Greek food and invited them to be the subject of a television program. At about the same time, Gary Hiebert, author of the Oliver Towne column in the *St. Paul Pioneer Press*, wrote a column about the Acropol. The media attention to the small struggling business gave them the exposure they needed to survive.

Aris and Cassandra and their four children: George, Christina, Vassiliki, and Dionysios, all worked in the restaurant. The parents, Aris and Cassandra, worked all day, every day, seven days a week from 6:00 A.M. until after midnight until one day in 1978 when their eldest son, George, sat them down in a booth for a serious talk. He pointed out to his parents that they had not attended his high school graduation

The Apostolou family in the dining room of the Acropol Inn Restaurant, 748 Grand Avenue. From left to right: Dionysius, Cassandra, Aris, and George. (Photo courtesy of Aris Apostolou.)

because they had had to work. With tears running down his face, he asked his parents, "What happened to our family? We children no longer have a mother and a father."

After that talk with George, Aris and Cassandra closed the Acropol restaurant on Sundays. Every other day of the week diners will find Cassandra working as hostess, Aris in the kitchen cooking and George and Dionysios, in formal attire, waiting on customers at the cloth-covered tables. George and Dionysios plan to continue the restaurant, consistently voted best Greek restaurant in the Twin Cities, into the next generation.[11]

The traditional restaurants are at the opposite extreme from most of the ethnic eateries. They are more expensive, offer full service, provide an extensive wine list and expect patrons to make reservations in advance.

The traditional restaurant most identified with Grand Avenue is the Lexington, known simply as "The Lex" to its patrons. The Lexington began life in October 1935 as a one-room neighborhood tavern serving beer, liquor, sandwiches, and popcorn. It had been purchased for $2,800 by Frank McLean, a distributor for a local brewery, who handed it over to his wife, Veronica, to run. Their bartender was an underage (for serving liquor) high school student named Don Ryan. When World War II broke out, Ryan joined the Marines. Lawrence Platt remembers the Lex during the war years as a diner serving California style hamburgers where host Frank McClain could always be counted on to produce a steak and some cigarettes for soldiers home on leave. After the war, Don Ryan came back to the Lexington for a tempo-

Don Ryan as Grand Old Day Grand Marshall in 1990. (*Highland Villager* photo.)

174

rary job that lasted for fifty-one years—until the restaurant was sold in 1991 to Rick Webb.

The story of the Lexington Restaurant is really the story of Veronica McLean and Don Ryan. According to Ryan, Veronica was a remarkable woman, exacting and meticulous in her standards, with a vision of the Lexington, not as a neighborhood bar, but as the best dining establishment in the Twin Cities. To achieve her goal, she hired the architect and designer Werner Wittkamp to redesign the restaurant on the order of a formal English Club. She lured accomplished chefs into the kitchen and she hired Don Ryan as manager.

For fifty years the business, professional and civic leaders of the Twin Cities dined at the Lexington. Hubert Humphrey, Walter Mondale, Rudy Perpich, Wendell Anderson, and the doctors Mayo all dined with some regularity at the Lex. Ryan remembers families who, as the occasions arose, celebrated engagements, weddings, the births of children, the children's graduations and marriages, and even meals after funerals at the Lexington.

The Lexington issued its own credit cards, and women who were regular diners could expect to receive Don Ryan's discreet peck on the cheek before he escorted them to

Entrance to the Lexington Restaurant. (Photo courtesy of Don Ryan.)

The Williamsburg Room of the Lexington Restaurant in 1985. (Photo courtesy of Don Ryan.)

The Lexington Restaurant dining room in 1942. (Photo courtesy of Don Ryan.)

their tables. He also solved unusual problems. One noon he observed an elderly woman and her two companions looking about them in an increasingly frantic way. When he inquired if he could be of help, they told him that grandmother had mislaid her false teeth. Without thinking, he asked if they were in her mouth, and, after a moment's hesitation, the elderly women discovered that they were.

Ryan learned so much about the regulars at the Lex that he knew when married partners were there with people other than their spouses. On many occasions, he steered diners away from rooms where their spouses were eating with others. One good customer came in with a girl friend and wanted to be seated in the bar, where, Ryan knew, his wife was having a drink with another man. Only by telling the customer that he wanted his advice on the lighting was Ryan able to persuade him to eat in the dining room with his companion. Under the management of Veronica McClain and Don Ryan, the Lexington Restaurant became a St. Paul institution, a formal, full-service, traditional restaurant that drew customers from across the entire Twin Cites region.[12]

Another type of restaurant to find a home on Grand Avenue is the contemporary restaurant. These establishments offer full service, but they are not formal. Diners feel at ease in any sort of attire (which would not be true of the Lexington), and prices are generally lower. Wait staff are dressed informally, and the clients are the upscale younger customers on Grand.

The fast food restaurants on Grand are typified by

The bar room of the Lexington Restaurant in 1941. (Photo courtesy of Don Ryan.)

high volume take-out food served on paper plates with plastic utensils. The retail restaurants are delis and other establishments that have a split personality—selling in bulk for take out and serving meals on the site.

The great diversity of restaurants on the avenue, from the most formal to the most casual, creates a special ambiance that brings customers back to the street. Most households can find an eating establishment on Grand to fit their mood and occasion.

There was a constant turnover in the restaurant business on Grand during the 1980s. Two or three restaurants would go out of business each year, and their places would be quickly taken by others with fresh ideas. By 1988, it was clear that Grand Avenue was on the verge of developing into an eating and entertainment district. Its potential was limited, however. The neighborhood residents objected to noisy patrons disrupting the serenity of the nearby streets, parking was scarce, and patrons driving in from the suburbs sometimes had difficulty locating Grand Avenue.

The newest presence on the street is that of the coffee houses. While the restaurants on Grand have always served coffee to their patrons, the coffee houses as a distinctive kind of cafe came to Grand with the opening of Dunn Brothers in 1986 at 1569 Grand. Ed Dunn and his brother Dan were living in Portland, Oregon, when they made plans to open a coffee shop and specialty bean roastery someplace in the United States. They decided against the West Coast as the coffee house phenomenon had already begun there.

After what Ed concedes was "minimal research,"

Grand Old Day parade watchers in front of Dunn Brothers Coffee House. (*Highland Villager* photo.)

178

they decided on St. Paul, although neither of them had ever been in the city before. Their first choice for space was on University Avenue, and, when they were unable to get the necessary permits for that location, they turned to the site on Grand Avenue. The space had previously housed a beauty salon, a religious book store, and the offices of a missionary group called "Camp Farthest Out." For $22,000 the Dunns were able to turn it into Grand's first coffee house.[13]

The Dunn brothers began the daily roasting of beans on the premises and the serving of variety coffees. The fragrance of roasting coffee beans wafted over the intersection. Soon students could be seen sitting at the sidewalk tables over a beverage and books, and a line of patrons that stretched down the sidewalk formed every morning for a cup of fresh roasted coffee.

The popularity of coffee and espresso coincided with the changing perception of Grand Avenue, namely that it was more than a traffic corridor—it was social space. Certain spaces along Grand became the living rooms and parlors for whomever wanted to occupy them.

Dunn's success with coffee demonstrated that a shop selling one specialty product could succeed on the street. Within nine years, eight coffee houses opened on Grand, five of them independent operations and three owned by franchises. When asked why coffee houses are so successful, Dunn shrugs and says, "It's a neighborhood kind of thing." He also credits their growth to the coming of age of a population that was not enamored with instant coffee, the residential density of the Grand neighborhood, and the high proportion of college-educated professional people. Dunn also credits a change in society to one that is more cosmopolitan in its orientation, more mature, more established in its cultural norms and has developed more sophisticated tastes.

Dunn Brothers coffee, the first coffee shop on Grand, at 1569 Grand Avenue. (Dave Lanegran photo.)

East wall of the Dunn Brothers Coffee shop at 1569 Grand. The wall was painted in the summer of 1994 by a group of local graffiti artists. (Dave Lanegran photo.)

These clients both observe and are part of the scene. Lingering over a cup of coffee, they read, write, work on projects on laptop computers or engage in conversation with other customers. As the lines between work and leisure blur, the coffee house serves many needs, as a second office in which to meet a client, as a place to study, to think, to work on a project, the place to play a game with total strangers, or just relax and watch the changing scene. When asked by Macalester geography students what drew patrons to a particular coffee house, the majority of the responses referred to the quality of the coffee and the shop's function as a place to meet with friends.

Coffee houses offer a form of social space different from bars. An invitation for a cup of coffee does not imply as much as an invitation to go out for drinks. This non-committal form of social encounter is important for those wanting to socialize without the risks of alcohol consumption. The coffee houses on Grand Avenue provide a degree of informal togetherness that one finds in village pubs in England or the sidewalk cafes in Italy.

Each coffee house has its group of regulars who prefer that establishment over the others for its special ambiance and product. Some like the more funky atmosphere of the independent shops; others frequent Starbucks or one of the two Caribou Coffee houses. The crowd that frequents coffee shops is not limited to one particular age group. While a large number of the customers are in their twenties and thirties, a high proportion are older clients buying beans in search of the perfect brew.

At Dunn Brothers, the major portion of the business is the sale of beans. Ed sells about 300 pounds of beans daily, seven days a week, at the Grand Avenue store, and most coffee sales are in the form of beans. (Dunn Brothers now has six coffee houses in the Twin Cities, but the Grand Avenue

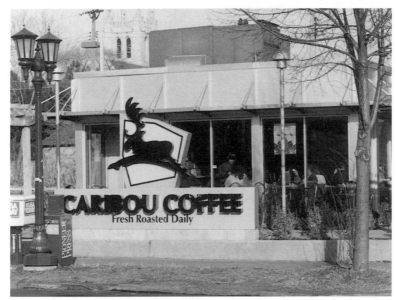

Caribou Coffee at 957 Grand Avenue. (Dave Lanegran photo.)

store makes the highest gross.)

The location of the coffee houses on Grand follows the distribution of the people. Furthest west is Cuppa Joe, catering principally to Macalester College students. Moving east is Dunn Brothers, then a Caribou Coffee Shop at Grand and Oxford, Cafe Con Amore at Milton Mall, Starbucks in Victoria Crossing East, Espresso Extra at 674 Grand, a second Caribou at 757 Grand, and Rosey's just east of Dale on Grand.

The second Caribou, four blocks east of Starbucks and less than a mile from the first Caribou, was intended to be a drive-in for patrons who would buy a mug of coffee to enjoy on their way to work The drive-in plans ran into objections from the Summit Hill Association, members of which were concerned that the traffic generated by the drive-in could become a nuisance on the street. Before the issue could be debated, however, it was settled when the owner of the land, Aris Apostolou, refused to give his permission.[14]

As in previous years, the merchants moving onto the avenue were attracted by the market potential in the surrounding neighborhoods. However, by the late 1980s, Grand was developing a strong image, and 235 of the newcomers indicated they were attracted by the nature of the street itself, independent of the neighborhoods. A 1985 study by the *St. Paul Pioneer Press/Dispatch* reported that 75,000 people shopped on the street in a thirty-day period. When the study's estimate was annualized, it indicated that about 900,000 people shopped on the street that year.[15]

The success of the street drove up land values, and, by 1988, seventy-three percent of the businesses were located in rental property. Gone were the days of the exclusively owner-occupied business community. The trade area of the merchant had not changed, but there were more establishments serving the suburban populations than previously.

All was not wonderful for the developers of the malls during this period. Jim Wengler had sold the first Victoria Crossing, Victoria Crossing West, and the parking lot to get financing for his other projects. He sold it to a husband and wife partnership formed by Laurel and James Crockeral. After holding the property for only a brief time, the Crockerals sold the building and parking lot in 1984 to Howard Bergerud, a Twin Cities developer, for one million nine hundred thousand dollars. Bergerud financed the deal for two million nine hundred thousand dollars, using tax exempt revenue bonds that had been made available to finance the rehabilitation of historic structures. The bonds were to pay eleven percent interest and came due on November 1, 1991.

This began a confusing period of complicated financial maneuvers by Bergerud and his associates that led through the courts and bankruptcy proceedings to the eventual ownership of three of the four Victoria Crossing malls by James Stolpestad, one of the four original young men who had purchased the first Victoria Crossing building in 1972 for $67,500.

Before buying Victoria Crossing West, Bergerud, in 1982, had purchased the opera company building (the one that Jim Wengler thought he had an option to buy) and renovated it into Victoria Crossing South. In 1985, he purchased the building at Grand and Milton and converted it into Milton Mall. He mortgaged the buildings to the hilt, and then raised rents to try to meet his payments. This had the effect of forcing rents up in all of the malls. In 1988, Bergerud sold Victoria Crossing West to a limited partnership managed by his partner, G. Craig Christensen. Forty investors bought three fourths of the eighty-two units at $14,750 each. Bergerud held 16.5 units, but reportedly only paid for five. Eighteen months later, he bought back the parking lot from the partnership for $695,000.

By the early 1990s disaster could not be forestalled. Taxes had not been paid on the buildings for four years, and the limited partners were threatening lawsuits. In the words of Jim Stolpestad, "Bergerud walked away from Milton Mall in 1990 and from the South Mall in 1992. He was forced out of the West Mall in 1992 and also lost the parking lot." In the legal proceedings that followed, Midwest Federal took over the West Mall, and Milton Mall was placed in bankruptcy. First Bank foreclosed on the parking lot.

Jim Stolpestad had been one of the limited partners in the Milton Mall development. When Bergerud abandoned the project, Stolpestad stepped in and took over the management in early 1992 and bought it in 1993. He took over the management of the South Mall in 1992 and ownership of that building in 1993. He purchased the West Mall in 1996. Kirtland Woodhouse bought the parking lot in 1994 and, to the consternation of the business owners at Victoria Crossing, converted it from a free to a pay parking lot.

In 1972, Wengler, Stolpestad, Smith, and Swardson had purchased the building that became Victoria Crossing West for $67,500. At the end of the 1970s any of the buildings at Grand and Victoria could have been purchased for a million to a million and one-half dollars. In the boom years between 1986 and 1989 they were valued at more than three million each. After the real estate crash of the late 1980s and early 1990s, the fair market value of the buildings is estimated to be in the mid two million dollars. Market forces, fluctuating interest rates, greed, and the Summit Hill Association all played a part in the drama of the malls on Grand Avenue.

As the twentieth century draws to a close, the quarter-century-old dream of an integrated social and shopping space at Grand and Victoria may become a reality after all. Few people understand the dynamics of the street and neighborhood better than Jim Stolpestad. His vision and ability may help insure that this particular urban space remains special.

Notes

1. Interview by Billie Young with Jim Solin, September 14, 1995.

2. *The Avenue 1995*, (St. Paul, Minnesota, Macalester College, 1995), pp. 8-9.

3. Interview by Billie Young with Paul Rudolph, September 19, 1995.

4. Interview by Billie Young with Don LaValle, October 15, 1995.

5. Interview by Billie Young with Charles and Harriet Fogarty, October 18, 1995.

6. *Grand Gazette*, June, 1991, p. 5.

7. Interview by Billie Young with Jim Wuollet, October 20, 1995.

8. Telephone interview by Billie Young with Lisbet Wolf, November 3, 1995.

9. *The Avenue 1987*, p. 76.

10. Ibid, p. 85.

11. Apostolou interview.

12. Interview by Billie Young with Don Ryan, October 14, 1995.

13. Interview by Billie Young with Ed Dunn, July 28, 1995.

14. Chris Trost.

15. *The Avenue 1993* (St. Paul, Minnesota, Macalester College), p. 76-78.

16. Howard Berg, *Corporate Report*, February, 1992, pp. 43-47.

17. Interview by Billie Young with James Stolpestad, August 17, 1995.

Commercial building at the corner of Grand and Hamline in the early 1970s. The businesses occupying the building in 1996 are, from left, Woodlines, Custom Crafted Upholstery, Grand Shanghai Restaurant and Express, Royal Tailor, Sixth Chamber Used Books, and Treadle Yard Goods. (Dave Lanegran photo.)

17

Franchises Find Grand Avenue

A CASUAL STROLL DOWN GRAND AVENUE or an investigation of its market potential raises a number of questions. The first is, "What is in a name?" Place names convey an atmosphere or sense of place. While not every establishment on the street uses the word "Grand" in its name, a great many do, and there are witty adaptations. They range from "Just Grand" to "Grand Groomers" and "Grand Paws" (pet shops) through "Grand Nails," "Baby Grand," "Grand Old Wash" (a laundromat), "Grand Jete," "Everything's Grand," "Grand Array," "Grand Spectacle," "Grand Cleaners," and "Grand Cafe" to the improbable "Grand Shanghai Express."

In the same way that suburban promoters used powerful images such as Eden Prairie, Roseville, and Highland Park, Wright and Wann have controlled our thinking about this street's destiny. They thought the street should be important, so Wann gave it a short, powerful, unambiguous name. Many people mistakenly call the grandiose boulevard one block north of the street "Grand." The name fits that street better than "Summit" does because, for most of its length, Summit Avenue is not on any sort of promontory. The name "Grand" helps create a positive image for the avenue. If it had a different name, such as Avon, Albert, or Dale, would people be so willing to ascribe special significance to it?

Grand Avenue is generally regarded as a successful street, but what does "success" really mean? For some property managers, it means a place with high rents and low vacancy rates. For others success means a locale where they

185

can stroll in safety through an interesting set of buildings, facades, and landscapes. For others success means a street offering places to live at low cost but that also has some style.

For some business people, a successful street is one where most of the business owners belong to the business association and cooperate and work together on projects, such as Grand Meander and Grand Old Day. They place a high value on joint projects that promote the street and foster an atmosphere of togetherness.

For nearby residents a successful street is one where they can get the goods and services they need quickly and conveniently and where the stores are run by owners who recognize them and cater to their needs. For almost everyone, a successful street is one that, when they are walking or driving on it, helps them feel good about themselves, where they are and what they are doing. Some of the criteria for a definition of success are mutually supportive, while others are contradictory. Some can be quantified, while others are very difficult to describe or even communicate.

While the old song may assert that "the best things in life are free," for most analysts, a measure of market value is the best test of success. Using the market value criteria and concentrating on the commercial space, the success of the avenue is undeniable. In the mid-1990s only one and one-half percent of the leaseable rental space stood vacant in the core area between Hamline and Dale. Grand Avenue was essentially fully leased.

The vacancy rate is obviously affected by the rental rate. Mall leases in the mid-1990s are somewhat lower than in the large suburban shopping malls but higher than some downtown St. Paul locations. Not all rents along the avenue are comparable to downtown, but all are higher than those on other commercial strips developed during the streetcar era. If we assume the rental market is an accurate reflection of the ability of entrepreneurs to make money at a business location, Grand is clearly successful.

The potential of the market served by Grand Avenue has been known locally for several years, but only in the early 1990s did the word about the avenue's success get out to national marketers. By the mid-1990s, national and regional chains had discovered Grand, and their operations constituted about one-third of all the businesses in the core area of the avenue. James Stopelstad believes that this is a healthy mix of local and non-local ownership. While the suburban malls and automobile-oriented shopping strips are developed according to formulas based on chain store operations and include almost no local ownership, there are no models for the local/non-local mix of businesses on commercial strips. The presence of both regional and national chain store operations complicates the picture of Grand.

For some observers, the presence of national chain stores means the street has joined the "big leagues." Like those who believe no city can be successful without professional sports clubs, the franchise advocates on Grand believe that the presence of the national chains legitimizes their claims about the value of the street. If Grand has attracted the attention of the major operators, it must be all right.

The presence of a few national chains has made dramatic changes to the streetscape. Pier One and Blockbuster Video bought and cleared their corner sites to make way for signature buildings. The Summit Hill Association approved a variance for Blockbuster Video to build its store out to the sidewalk, significantly changing the appearance of the intersection. The build-out was opposed by the parks department. The association had one request, that Blockbuster put a functioning clock in its clock tower. Whole Foods signifi-

Pier 1 Imports at 733 Grand Avenue. (Dave Lanegran photo.)

The Datsun dealership at 733 Grand Avenue where Pier 1 is now located. (Dave Lanegran photo.)

Blockbuster Video store on the northeast corner of Grand and Lexington, showing the clocks the Summit Hill Association requested be put in the tower. (Dave Lanegran photo.)

cantly remodeled an existing grocery store, but its building merely succeeded another supermarket that had been on that site and did not materially change the appearance of the street. With a few notable exceptions, the chains on Grand Avenue are regional operations that require comparatively small store fronts. Aside from their distinctive signage and coloration, most blend into the streetscape.

For other observers of Grand Avenue, the arrival of the national and regional chains is not good. They see it as a growing trend away from local control, the expression of peculiar local interests and thus the erosion of the uniqueness of Grand. Steve Lyon laments the departure of the smaller independently owned stores from the street, believing they are the institutions that give the street its special ambiance and character. He also notes that the owners of the small independent businesses were the ones who organized the street events, worked on the Grand Old Day committees and served on the Grand Avenue Business Association.

Managers of the chain stores are noticeably absent from the rosters of volunteers who run Grand Meander and Grand Old Day. Absentee corporate owners seem to be unaware of and disinterested in festival events on a distant street where they own a business. And it is not in the job descriptions of franchise store managers to spend their evenings and weekends in meetings helping organize street fairs or planning joint promotions with other businesses on the street. As a result, the chain stores, despite their greater resources, do not provide leadership or support for the activities on Grand.

The chain stores contradict the generally held belief that the success of Grand is dependent upon the special relationships between clients and owners. Critics of the franchises argue that these relationships cannot be provided by the teenagers and young adults employed by absentee owners and managers, and they fear that, over time, Grand Avenue will become just another suburban franchise row.

The Great Harvest Bakery at 1049 Grand Avenue is an example of a franchise business that "fits" on Grand. The owner, Bonnie Johnson, can be found most days in her store, dressed in a white apron and with flour on her nose. She is active in the Grand Avenue Business Association and was co-chair with Brian Alton of the 1996 Grand Old Day event.

Franchises are a recent innovation in American culture. Architectural critics point out that it was during the 1960s that American retailing entered the franchise era. At first the franchisers led retailers away from building idiosyncratic structures such as buildings shaped like hot dogs, wedges of cheese and teepees. The franchisers stressed simple, recognizable forms and colors. Neon was replaced with back-lighted signs made of brightly colored plastic. Great attention was paid to detail and design quality.

In the 1970s and 1980s, the companies continued their search for crisp memorable images that could be called a reflection of a new style. As a result, the chains introduced more subdued designs, and the McDonald golden arches began to shrink. These new designs are highly finished and have a pleasant appearance. However, they clearly lack vitality and individuality. Their relative sameness is punctuated by strong corporate logos and signs, company colors, and, in some cases, building styles. This style gives the new sections of all American cities the look of having been put together with interchangeable parts. A visitor to these streets has no clues as to what city he is in. It could as well be Cleveland or

Grand Avenue in the 1970s (above) with the Kentucky Fried Chicken franchise at 769 Grand in the background. This view of Grand shows what neighbors feared would happen to the entire avenue. (Dave Lanegran photo.)

Grand Spectacle (right) in the remodeled Kentucky Fried Chicken building at 769 Grand. (Dave Lanegran photo.)

189

Walgreens and Victorian
lights on Grand, 1990.
(*Highland Villager* photo.)

Indianapolis. These same parts are now being used in Australia, Great Britain, Canada, and other suburban landscapes around the world.

Grand Avenue observers wonder how these interchangeable parts can add to the character and remarkable sense of place that exists on Grand Avenue. The developers and merchants active on Grand in the 1970s promoted historic preservation and romantic themes to distinguish the street from its competition. They used images of the past to try to convince shoppers that the street was special and, as on main streets of the past, that the customers and merchants here had a special set of relationships.

Can the slick suburban architecture of the turn of the twentieth century maintain those place images in people's minds? While no one is calling for Dominos, Pier One, Walgreens, and Blockbuster Video to relocate, questions

The Green Mill at Grand
and Hamline. (Dave
Lanegran photo.)

about the impact of more franchise-designed storefronts and fluorescent lighted interiors remain close to the surface in conversations on the street.

A more fundamental criticism of the growth of franchises on Grand comes from those who are wary of the "commodification" of our culture and neighborhoods. For the Canadian author James Lorimer, "The Corporate City" is not so much a place for people to live and call their own as it is a machine rationally and effectively designed to make money. In the corporate city there is a great deal of rhetoric about community, family, and neighborhood, but, in actuality, each aspect of life is separated and retooled for greater profit.[1]

The entire process is overlain with images of fun and romance. These images are necessary to hide the colorless reality of much of everyday life. The process behind all this is "commodification" which means that every aspect of life is viewed as a commodity, a product that can be marketed, packaged and sold to make money and ensure the survival of the corporation. Anything, from national history and sexual fantasies, to local history and family life can be "imagineered."

Most aspects of commodification are pleasant enough. After all, no sales manager wants his product to be off-putting. The old is blended with the new in forms of architecture sometimes referred to as "nouveaux-old." But at the heart of it, all the lines between reality and fiction are

The Subway Shop at 1820 Grand on the site of a former drugstore. The billboard on the roof illustrates the contrast between generic advertising versus site-specific signage. (Dave Lanegran photo.)

blurred. Places become generic. History, imagination, and invention become inseparable.

The corporate city is popular and pervasive in newly developed areas. Those who speak out against it must be careful because their objections can be construed to be abstract complaints about convenient places that are also safe and pleasant. Nevertheless, commodification of the landscape results in the dilution of the sense of place and the meaning of landscapes.

In addition, the corporate city results in a dramatic diminution of choices. The corporate city with its commodified life styles is very seductive and successful. People shop in malls owned and managed by corporations, live in residential suburbs developed according to hierarchical corporate styles and work in corporate skyscrapers or office parks. They go to and from these landscapes via limited access highways. For some it is impossible to imagine a future not dominated by the mass-produced, interchangeable corporate landscapes.

Fortunately, the complete transformation of older cities into corporate landscapes has not yet occurred. Some places thought to be unprofitable by the developers will be ignored, and there are pieces of older cities that have yet to be transformed. Grand Avenue is one such place. Grand Avenue has not become a corporate landscape despite its commercialization. While the franchises are introducing their interchangeable buildings and storefronts, the street is still not owned by a few large corporations. There is more to Grand than the minimalls. The mixture of land uses and

The Ramaley building at 666 Grand, showing how a portion of the building was taken down for a parking lot. (Dave Lanegran photo.)

building types is the opposite of the uniformities of the corporate vision for suburbs and downtowns. It is this heterogeneity that makes Grand Avenue what it is.

Corporate landscapes are dominated by patriarchal hierarchies that demand calm conformity. Deviations from expected behavior are discouraged, and the corporate watchmen enforce the rules of behavior. Cameras are always watching. While Grand Avenue is protected by city police and employees of various establishments, it is still a democratic place. A wide variety of behaviors is tolerated and even encouraged. Because the street is not all commercial, one need not be shopping to enjoy the ambiance of the place. Likewise, because it is not all housing one need not be a resident or a guest to use the sidewalks.

The sidewalks distinguish Grand from the suburban shopping strips and malls. They are public space, though a few coffeeshops and restaurants have claimed pieces of them for their patrons. Even though businesses along the street have adapted to the automobile, the presence of sidewalks and pedestrians clearly states that the machine does not rule the landscape. There are other options, and walking and biking are encouraged. Bill Wengler gave up one of his cherished parking spaces at Victoria Crossing East to put in a bicycle rack.

The small scale operations that typify Grand hearken back to a time before the 1960s when franchises began to play a dominant rule in retailing. Grand in the 1990s, in many ways, reflects where the rest of the country was in the 1960s when franchises accounted for only about thirty percent of the total retail business in the United States.

The ambiance created by smaller local owners is undoubtedly what people consider when they describe Grand Avenue as being like the main street of a small town. What they are remembering are cities of the mid-twentieth century. The metaphor of the small town is used because it is recognized that the structure of the commercial community on Grand is different from the sort of business that dominates the current economy. While customers and visitors really do not think of Grand Avenue as a small town main street, they do recognize that it is an older form of commercial landscape.

For those who value the special atmosphere of Grand Avenue, the increase in the number of franchise operations is an ambiguous event. Their presence is a sign of economic health, and they bode well for continued good maintenance of the other buildings along the avenue.

On the other hand, the arrival of the national chains may be the first phase of the commodification of Grand

Avenue. There is no research on the movement of franchises onto commercial strips already dominated by independent or local chain stores. James Stolpestad is correct in his observation that the mixture of chains and independent stores makes the Grand Avenue commercial community robust. Ample evidence also suggests that the franchise architecture can be blended into the heterogeneous streetscape of Grand Avenue. However, the razing of structures to make way for franchise architecture has begun, and dramatic changes may lay ahead.

The time for design guidelines for the avenue has arrived. Recent surveys of the business operators on Grand indicate that the majority of them have located there because of the street's atmosphere. Linda Quinn applies her "squint eye test" to a business to determine if it meets her visual standard for a presence on Grand Ave. She is particularly opposed to fluorescent lighting in stores, claiming that this type of illumination can be deadly for a store, creating a cold environment, one she condemns as the "fast food look."

Shoppers and residents also indicate that the mixed use and special ambiance of the street are its main attractions for them. All three groups are expressing a desire to work, shop and live alternatively to the hierarchical corporate landscapes of the suburbs and downtowns. Therefore, steps should be taken to protect the street from gradual suburbanization and from being taken over by national chain stores. Unless this is done, it will not be easy for Grand Avenue to retain its very special character.

Grand Avenue does not exist in isolation. The street is connected to a variety of places throughout the metropolitan area. While design guidelines and other measures may help maintain the appearance of Grand Avenue, events occurring elsewhere in the city and in the neighborhoods combine with change on the street to have a great impact on developments on Grand. Many significant trends are simply outside the control of the merchants and developers working on the avenue.

For example, on January 11, 1996, Michelle Cromer Poire announced that, "with a heavy heart," she was closing Odegard Books of St. Paul. After eighteen years in business at Victoria Crossing on Grand Avenue, and after having been named "best independent bookstore" in the region, the store was forced to close by the combination of the competition of the chain bookstores Barnes and Noble, the permit parking in the neighborhood, and the conversion of the Victoria Crossing parking lot from a free to a pay lot.

Beginning in 1991, the Barnes and Noble company opened nine large bookstores in the Twin Cities trade area—three of them within a few miles of Odegard Books. The effect of these stores on Odegard's, which had become a regional bookstore, was to steadily erode sales from customers outside the Grand Avenue neighborhood. Michelle believes that the sales decline from this competition had ended and that the store was beginning to rebound when pay parking went into effect on the lot at Grand and Victoria. She traces the store's final decline to that event and the fact that parking on neighborhood streets was also closed to shoppers.

The closing of the Odegard store, one of the most popular and well-managed bookstores in the region, illustrates the symbiotic relationship that exists between a neighborhood and a commercial street. Actions taken to relieve one problem, in this case parking on neighborhood streets, may have long-term effects on the economic health of the commercial street in the neighborhood. The departure of Odegard Books will have a profound effect on the remaining businesses on the street and will change the "ethos" of Grand Avenue.

Note

1. James Lorimer, *The Developers*, (Toronto: J. Lorimer, 1978), p. 79.

The 1991 Grand Avenue Business Association officers and board. Back row: Mike Mischke, Dave Wildmo, Greg Roedler, Lane Peterson, Bill Skally, Dirk Dantuma, Michelle Poire Cromer, and Jim Rouleau. Front row: Carol Austermann, Mella Martin, Susan Vaas (entertainer for the evening), Bob McClay, Mimi Doran, and Billie Young. (*Highland Villager* photo.)

18

Elements of Grand's Success

PEOPLE INTERESTED IN CHANGING the character of a street frequently come to Grand Avenue in St. Paul, Minnesota, seeking ideas. They want to learn from the history of Grand Avenue the strategies and techniques that help commercial streets, especially those in the inner city, succeed.

The planning departments of almost every city in the country, as well as that of St. Paul, have worked to develop new commercial activity and to expand the existing business base in the older sections of cities in an effort to create jobs for residents and to improve the tax base. These efforts have had only limited success. Therefore, answers to questions about the reasons for Grand Avenue's success are significant. Are there elements of the Grand Avenue experience that may have relevance for other inner city streets in other places? And if so, what are they?

Before explaining Grand Avenue, however, we have to describe it. Once described we may be able to determine which components of the street can be transferred to other locations and situations. We believe the following features are key aspects of Grand Avenue's location and history.

(1) Grand Avenue has a good location. From the very first, it was a commercial street for a middle and upper class set of neighborhoods. The team of Wright and Wann envisioned Grand Avenue as the service street for the mansions along Summit and the large houses of the upper middle class families that would settle in Summit Park and Crocus Hill.

By laying down the streetcar tracks a century ago, they secured for Grand a favored position in the urban landscape. All kinds of activity would be attracted to the street because of its accessibility. It was easy to get to Grand. Other streets would also get streetcar lines, but Grand had a head start, and its early development insured that it would always have good mass transit, whether it was by trolley or by bus. Thus the street was well-connected to the moneyed households nearby, to downtown and to the middle class households closer to the city's western edge. Although the growth of more distant suburbs and the decline of downtown St. Paul hurt Grand Avenue, the fundamental strength of its position in the city enabled it to withstand the negative pressures until large scale reinvestment began.

(2) Neither the merchants nor the residents totally abandoned the street. While there were vacancies in specific buildings, rents were low, and buildings undervalued, there was always a market for the commercial and residential space. During the 1950s and 1960s, when the economy of the inner city began to turn down, Grand Avenue was still dominated by well-established businesses. Though many of these would go out of business or relocate, their departure was slow. For example, the car dealers did not all go at once. The mature small businessmen who lived in the neighborhood were not all prepared to pack up and move their operations.

As other parts of the city became devalued, there was a growing appreciation of Grand, and businesses relocated to the street to take advantage of available storefronts. The

The Grandview Theater at 1830 Grand was built in 1924 in an art deco style that has not changed over the seventy years it has served as a neighborhood entertainment center. (Dave Lanegran photo.)

presence of questionable businesses like the Red Carpet Sauna did not provoke community-wide hysteria and out-migration. Any negative impact the business might have had on its neighbors was quickly contained and a reasonable accommodation reached.

(3) Grand's renaissance was part of a general movement by the middle class to regain old middle class neighborhoods in St. Paul, the Twin Cities and across the country. The renovation of Grand ran with, not against, national trends. Although the individuals engaged in all phases of the rebuilding of Grand Avenue were innovators, they were not alone. The residential communities on each side of the street were discovered by ambitious people interested in forging a new lifestyle in St. Paul's core neighborhoods. The "back to the city" movement, historic preservation, and gentrification all fitted Grand Avenue perfectly.

This is an important feature because the street and the neighborhoods changed together. In some instances, the merchants and landowners along Grand clearly led. In other cases they followed ideas developed in the surrounding neighborhoods. After some initial reluctance, the merchants soon adopted Roger Swardson's Victorian concept for the shops and an old fashioned commercial community.

(4) At several crucial times in Grand's history, a group of individuals, principally from the small business community, developed an understanding of Grand Avenue and a vision for its future. These people were the engines of Grand Avenue's development. They were able to articulate that sense of place and vision and to convince a wide variety of individuals to embrace the image. Once the vision was understood and accepted, a variety of operational plans was developed to make the vision a reality.

There have been several groups of visionaries over the years. After Wright and Wann and the real estate devel-

Townhouses under construction on the west end of Grand Avenue during the winter of 1995-1996. Their construction exhibits the continued demand for housing on the street. (Dave Lanegran photo.)

opers, there were the leaders of Macalester College and Bishop Ireland who insisted on stretching the rails to the end of the Mississippi gorge. After them came the many builders and merchants who comprised the building blocks of the community.

In the crucial post-war years, the Grand Avenue Business Association led by Wally Peters, Doc Chopp, and others kept the faith in the future of the business community. They were joined by entrepreneurs like Mary Rice and the GABA executive, Mimi Doran, who eloquently articulated and worked for the vision of a three-mile-long business community. The entrepreneurs were joined by communicators like Roger Swardson, Elberta Matters, Mike Mischke, and the architect James Wengler who clearly saw the transition from a string of store fronts to the nodes of development around mini malls. None of this would have worked had not the investors like Don Dick at the First Bank Grand supported the dreams and schemes of the developers and merchants. Today Jim Stolpestad leads the street's development.

(5) The officialdom of the city acted to support the vision by developing laws and finance programs and by trying to be innovative when existing rules promised to defeat the vision. The first great stride forward was made possible when the street's business leaders and councilmen insisted on an equitable rezoning. The new map of the 1970s gave confidence to all sorts of investors. Business people were assured of room to grow and the lack of an artificial limit on commercial space meant that rents would not skyrocket because of a lack of rentable space.

The Wedding Shoppe at 1196 Grand Avenue. Note the connection between the two buildings. (Dave Lanegran photo.)

In addition, the apartment houses were protected. The several planning and design studies, especially the one that produced the B-2C zoning, insured that the best ideas of the professional community were made available to the local population working on Grand. When there was a clear need to change the rule, the planning department staff came up with the solution.

Thanks to the B-2C zoning decision, Jim and Lois Fritz may have the only wedding shop in the country that is located in four separate houses, all of them former single family homes. The interiors of the houses have been changed, but the exteriors have remained the same. The Fritzes opened their first Wedding Shoppe in 1977 at 1196 Grand in a house with about 2,000 square feet of space. When the house across the street at 1201 became available, they bought it and moved in their custom fitting department. In 1992, they added a third house, the residence at 1197 Grand, and, in April 1995, they bought the fourth at 1192.

According to Jim, customers are not disturbed by the unconventional setting and "love the home-type atmosphere of the houses." Buyers now come from a five-state area, and the business has become one of the most successful wedding stores in the United States. "The beauty of Grand Avenue," says Jim, "is that customers from all over know where it is."[1]

(6) Individuals developed a sense of ownership in the success of Grand Avenue and acted on that sense of belonging. Scores of individuals risked their life savings on Grand. Some stood up in public meetings and argued with the representatives of big business. Some put up large sums of money to build what they thought would be excellent social space. From Doc Chopp calling the bluffs of petty thugs to Nancy Fish housing the Grand Old Day horses in her backyard, the firm sense of place held by individuals evoked actions that have combined to make that shared vision a reality for all of the residents of the metropolitan area.

(7) A relatively open democratic process emerged over the years to deal with the issues confronting the development of the street. The several organizations representing the neighborhoods and the merchant community provided a forum for the expression of views and critiques of what was happening on the street. In addition, the editors of the *Grand Gazette* played the role of gadfly and constantly reminded residents, owners, and shoppers of their duty to maintain a strong community. Later development of community councils insured that discussions of developments would all be held in public. No organization, not even the wealthy private

colleges, can unilaterally change conditions along Grand Avenue.

(8) Small- and middle-scale entrepreneurs were able to become part of the economy of the street. The initial sub-division of the land into lots of standard city size made the assemblage of large parcels for development costly and time consuming. George Buck had to resort to subterfuge to assemble a piece of land large enough for a used car lot.

All of the small frontage lots produced small store fronts. The small commercial spaces meant small operations could move in without paying the high fees of the malls. In a sense, the small spaces acted as incubators. Yet unlike city-sponsored incubators in rehabilitated industrial locations, these spots were in the midst of a great market. The presence of small scale entrepreneurs guarantees diversity, innovation, and refreshing change. They are the essence of urban life.

(9) The local bank was able to spur and encourage reinvestment on the street after the entrepreneurs proved the worth of the location. It is not possible to measure the amount of money First Bank Grand turned over in the community. Clearly Don Dick's decision to seek out loans in the area and to send signals to other banks that Grand was First Bank territory gave the merchants on the street a competitive edge. While not everyone will agree with all of the bank's decisions, no one will argue the fact that the bank played a critical rule in the redevelopment process. First Bank Grand was not the only financial institution on the street (Cherokee Bank opened a branch in an attractive new building at 895 Grand in 1986 under president James Gesell), but it was the most visible.

(10) The street has kept crime under control. Foot patrolmen walk the beat. The street has not attracted loiter-ers of the sort who threaten pedestrians and shoppers. There are no drunks sleeping off a night's carousing on the bench-es at the bus stops, no castoff liquor bottles or refuse in the gutters. Grand Avenue sidewalks are spaces where rules of personal conduct are, for the most part, self-enforced. They are like public streets used to be before any misbehavior was tolerated.

Change is constant and there have been failures as well as successes. The great issue is what direction change will take. There is no way to determine the exact number of people who have lived on the avenue, nor can we know how many people have operated businesses there. The statistics clearly indicate there have been many. Some businesses have enjoyed success for several decades. These flagship institutions have been joined by hosts of newcomers who are spreading their wings in the supportive commercial culture.

While change is constant, there are important directions. The first is that businesses have grown in size as well as in number. Square footage has increased, dollar volume has grown, and the size of the market area has increased. Grand is no longer a neighborhood shopping street, although it serves the needs of the neighborhood. It is now an entertainment and special shopping district of some magnitude. While the ups and down of the American economy have clearly impacted the street, the depressions and recessions have not broken it. The economy of Grand has not stagnated, and the residential areas have been modernized to match the accommodations available elsewhere in the metro area. Fortunately, the fads of shopping and building have not swept away the accomplishments of the past. Change has occurred, but the change has reinforced confidence in the future. The many successes of Grand have attracted additional creative people to both live and work there.

In August 1995, a newcomer to the Twin Cities came to Grand Avenue for the first time. She had been told that she might find the street interesting, and, if she had time, it would be worth a visit. Acting on that advice, she drove to St. Paul, parked near Victoria Crossing, and started out on what she thought would be a pleasant sojourn that would last no more than two hours. One happy surprise lead to another. A casual conversation lead to a series of informal discussions with clerks, shopowners, and customers. She was hooked.

Before the day was over, she had located several shops and restaurants on the avenue she wanted to revisit and was making plans to return frequently with her friends. While the details of this event are not duplicated by the reactions of all visitors to the street, the essential story is. Visitors—whether they are freshmen at the neighborhood colleges, students at William Mitchell College of Law, Grand Old Day visitors, suburbanites, neighbors, architects, or sophisticated urban planners—are all smitten by the street.

Some are able to articulate the source of their pleasure. Others do not know the name for it, but they know what they like. Two years after the closing of the Old Mexico Shop, people still call the owners to lament its passing. What they are missing, as much as that particular store, is the presence on the street of a personal, idiosyncratic business statement. It is these individual expressions of passions and interests—be they florists in a yellow Victorian house with statuary in the front yard, sellers of rare prints with a bird sanctuary in the backyard, or a shoe repair shop that sharpens ice skates—that give Grand Avenue its remarkable sense of place.

That intuitive understanding in people's minds of what is appropriate for the street and what is not, may, in the end, be its greatest protection and its greatest asset. So long as the owners and users of the land along the street are able to apply Linda Quinn's "squint eye test," to adapt the trends in the general economy to Grand's peculiar and authentic sense of place, the street will continue to be a source of pleasure and delight to all of the people who come to it.

Note

1. Telephone interview by Billie Young with James Fritz, September 16, 1995. The latest purchase, the house at 1192 Grand Avenue, was joined to the house at 1196 by a two-storey addition. The modification met with the approval of the Summit Hill Association.

Appendix

Grand Avenue Business Association
Presidents

Bonnie Johnson	Great Harvest Bakery	1997
Brian Alton	McClay, Alton Law Offices	1996
Deb Kowalski	Kowalski's Grand Market	1995
Bill Skally	Skally's Tax Service	1993-94
Pat Crowns	First Bank Grand	1993
Matt McDonough	Grand Spectacle	1992
Bob McClay	McClay, Alton Law Offices	1991
Billie Young	Old Mexico Shop	1990
Jim Wuollet	Wuollet Bakery	1988-89
Norm Geiger	Home Team Realtor	1986-87
Jim Solin	Grand Avenue Ace Hardware	1984-85
Don Bober	Bober Drug	1982-83
Harvey Giese	Grandview Barber Shop	1980-81
Jane Tiegen	The Basket Shoppe	1978-79
E. Peter Willwerscheid	Willwerscheid Mortuary	1976-77
John Rockney	Nelson Interiors	1974-75
Bob Hylton	Macalester Picture Framing	1972-73
Ray Meyer	First Bank Grand	1970-71
Dr. William Chopp	Dr. William Chopp, dentist	1968-69
Cy Seller	Green Mill	1966-67
Don Smolik	Grand Avenue Ace Hardware	1964-65
Wally Peters	Wally Peters Color Key	1962-63

Grand Avenue Business Association
Executive Directors

Charlotte Mason	January 1, 1996 -
Mary Capra	June 1, 1994 - December 1, 1995
Bill Patton	January 1, 1993 - June 1, 1994
Ann Geiser	June 1, 1992 - December 31, 1992
Kay Woitas	April 1, 1991 - May 31, 1992
Mimi Doran	1987 - March 31, 1991
Irene deVinney	
Ernie Winter	

Index

Abbott Paint 161
Ace Hardware 135
Acropol 123, 172
Alexander Ramsey School 21
American Bar and Grill 109
Andahazy Ballet 158
Andreas 13
Angus Hotel 29
Apartment buildings 29, 70
Apostolou, Aris and Cassandra 123
Archbishops 77
Avon Street 36

Back to the Cities Movement 82
Bailie, Ned 27
Baird, Julian 56
Banners 146
Barnes, Lucille 92
Barnes and Noble 195
Belco Company 37
Benedictine Sisters 76
Benner Lunch Box Company 44
Bergerud, Howard 111, 153, 182
Bibelot Shop 121
Blockbuster Video 188
Bober, Don 94
Boeckmann House 78
Bond, J. Wesley 9
Boss, Andrew 103

Brack, Myrtle 42
Bread and Chocolate 153
Bremer, Edward 50
Briar Patch 109
Broadway Street 17
Brotchner, Mr. 36
Buck, George 87, 105-106, 202
Bus 55

Cable car 17
Cafe Latte 32, 154
Cahn, Howard 50
Caldwell Banker 126
Cambridge Street 21
Caribou Coffee 181
Cathcart, Rebecca Marshall 9
Cavendar 13, 21
Charlemagne Jewelry Store 160-161
Chatsworth Street 36
Children's Hospital 122
Chopp, Barbara 89, 83
Chopp, Dr. William (Doc) 89, 91, 93, 130, 133, 137, 200
Ciatti's 32
Citizen's Ice and Fuel Company 38
Clapp Thomssen Agency 102, 105
Cleveland Avenue 19
Cleveland, Horace W. S. 11-12
Clothes to Boot 109

Cochran, Thomas 18-19
Coffee and Tea Ltd. 109
Collier's Weekly 55
Collins, Officer Dan 90
Commercial building 44
Creative Kids Stuff 147
Cretin Avenue 21, 42
Criminals 47-49
Crockeral, James and Laurel 182
Crocus Hill Market 33, 34
Crocus Hill Drug Store 102, 109
Crocus Hill 56, 79, 95, 197
Cromer, Michele Poire 146, 195
Crowns, Pat 116
Crumm, Bill 125
Cullen, Officer Mike 46
Cushing, Dunn and Driscoll Realtors 28

Dale Street 11, 17, 29, 34, 36, 79, 139
Dayton Avenue 9, 68
de Lauwe, Chombart 3
Dean, Judith Neren 149
Delivery men 39
Denzer, Peter 140
DeVinney, Irene 94, 124
DeWitts Beauty Shop 102, 104
Dick, Donald 103, 113, 117, 202
Dick, a man 42
Dickman, Gustav 36
Dietz, Mr. 36
Dillinger, John 1, 41, 47, 51
Diocesan Teachers College 76
District Planning 73
Donnelly Atlas 12-13, 19, 21
Doran, Mimi 94, 123, 200
Duluth Avenue 17
Dunn, John W. G. 27, 28
Dunn, William 50
Dunn Brothers 179

Edina Realty 28
Eldredge, Frank A. 23
Electric car 31
Erdahl, Carol 146
Esteban's 111

Fairview Avenue 17, 34
Finn, William 14
First Bank Grand 106, 113, 117
Fish, Nancy 123-125, 148

Fitzgerald Condominiums 80
Fitzgerald, F. Scott 1, 30
Flor, Henry H. 28
Fogarty, Charles W. and Harriet K. 161
Fohlmester, Lucille 117
Fort Snelling 21
Fourth Street 17
Franchises 185-195
Francis, Margaret 161
Franciscian Sisters 77
Freeman, Gov. Orville 63
Freese, Roxanne 148
Fritz, Wendell 86-87, 160
Fritz, Jim and Lois 201
Fur Trade 7

Galtier, Fr. Lucian 5
Garden of Eden 108
Garuda 108
Gehan, Mark 32, 51
Geiger, Norm 94
Gerdes, Cynthia 147
Gilbert's Tea Room 28
Goat cart 39
Gorbachev, Mikhail 127
Gobolish, Jim 87
Goodhue, James 6
Goodrich, Dr. Calvin Gibson 16
Goodrich Avenue 14, 35, 50, 79
Grand Avenue Business Association, 86, 89,
    101, 133, 139, 197
Grand Avenue Business Association, Incorporators
    88
Grand Avenue State Bank 103
Grand Gazette 101, 104, 140
Grand and Fairview intersection 52
Grand Avenue Liquor Store 86
Grand Avenue Market 1
Grand Avenue Grocery 33-34
Grand Hill 92
Grand Meander 119
Grand Old Day Committee 1989 129
Grand Old Day 121, 130
Grand Spectacle 190
Grand Wheeler II 137
Grandendale Drug Store 42
Grandendale Pharmacy 158
Grandview Theater 198
Granzberg, Grace 40
Great Harvest Bakery 189

Green, Charles 54
Green Mill 191
Griggs Street 13
Grotto Street 21, 36

Häagen Dazs 153
Hamline Auto Body Shop 96
Hamline Avenue 13, 21
Hamm, William Jr. 49
Harrold, George 60
Hayden, Mon. Ambrose 69, 78
Heath Plus 104
Hell's Kitchen 68
Hiebert, Gary 47, 173
High Winds Fund 166
Hill Seminary 21
Hill, James J. 76
Historic Preservation 70, 71, 75
Historic Hill District 73, 75
Hoffman, Mary E. 30, 41
Hogan, Dapper Danny 45
House tours 80-81
House of Hope 9
Housing and Redevelopment Authority 67
Howard, Timothy 62
Howe, Carol 145
Howell Street 139
Hozza, Dave 138
Huber, George 97
Hulfman, Jim 106
Hylton, Bob 94

Interstate 94 59
Ireland, Bishop John 5, 18, 19, 76
Irving Elementary School 21

Jacob Scmidt Brewing Company 50
James, Don 98
Jane Wilder Prest's Yarn Shop 102
Jefferson, Rufus 28
Jewish migration 57
Johnson McClay Law Office 128

Kaemmer, Martha 119
Keenan, Shirley 149
Kentucky Fried Chicken 190
Kit Connection 108
Kittson, Norman 76
Klein's Super Market 34
Kling, Lea 120

Knechtges, Dr. Venton W. 102
Koch, Bertha 117
Koehner 104
Koenig's Bakery 29
Kohner and Fredric Florists 102
Kowalski, Jim and Mary Ann 151
Kowalski, Bob 124
Kowalski's Market 123

Lacher Drug Store 36
Lanegran, David 134
Lanpher, Rollin A. 9
Larry's Dairy 85
Latimer, George i-ii
Laurel Avenue 10, 80
LaVahn, James 161
LaValle, Don 159
Lein, Max 117
Lexington Avenue 11, 13, 14, 18, 27, 36, 40, 41, 50
Lexington Restaurant 114, 175-176
Lietzow, Mr. 36
Lincoln Avenue 41
Lloyd's Automotive Service 159
Loan Programs 82
Lorimer, James 191
Lowry, Thomas 15-18
Lucky, Mr. 48
Lynden, James 82
Lyon, Steve 130, 189

Macalester College 2, 18, 21, 22, 29, 95, 101, 113, 123, 164
Malarky's Candy and Bakery 38
Market House 98, 99
Marson and Simonton 13
Martin Luther King Jr. Community Center 68
Massey, Jr., Reverend Floyd 62, 63
Matters, Elberta 115, 140, 200
McClay, Bob 94
McDonough, Matt 123
McGuire, Charles (Chuck) 137
McKasy, Maureen and Mary Pat 148
McLean, Veronica 175
McLeod, Bob 42
Merrian, John 20
Merrill, Giles W. 10
Milton Street 31, 34, 364
Milton Mall 118
Mini Malls on Grand 170
Minneapolis Street Railway Co. 16

Minnesota Opera Company 111
Mischke, Mike 124, 125, 147, 200
Mississippi River Blvd. 57
Mississippi River 11
Moonshine 47
Muska, Bill 162
Muska's Lighting Center 87, 162
Myers, Ray 91

Nath, Margaret 53
Neighborhood Change 70
Neil, Rev. Edward Dufield 9
Nonaka, Nori 161
Northwest Magazine 18, 22
Norton, L. Stolpp (Slunky) 40
Norton, Fred 89

O'Connor System 45
O'Connor, Richard 45
O'Connor, John J. 45
O'Connor System 49
Oakland Avenue 9, 92
Odegard Books, 107, 196
Odegard, Dan and Michelle 107
Old Mexico Shop 94, 97, 120
Old Town Restorations 80, 44, 153
Oldest Commerical Building on Grand 84
Olson, Craig 104
Olson, Martin 162
Olson's Bakery 40
Ossanna, Fred A. 54
Ox cart 7-8
Oxford Club 26-28, 40
Oxford Mall 159
Oxford Theater 40-41
Oxford Street 36

Paperback Traders 154
Parking 142, 144
Pascal Street 23
Payne, Jerry 125
Perpich, Governor Rudy 127
Peters, Otto G. 27
Peters, Wally 86, 87, 91, 200
Pier 1 Imports 188
Piggly Wiggly 29, 34, 167
Platt, Lawrence 38
Platt, Laura 40
Pont's Tea Room 28
Port's Tea Room 86, 87

Portland Avenue 54
Professor Baker's Dance Class 30
Prospect Park 60

Queen Contests 91, 145
Quinn, Linda 147, 194
Quinn, Peter 127, 152

Radio Girl Perfume Company 37
Ramaley Company 29
Ramaley Hall 30-31
Ramaley Building 193
Ramsey County 12
Ramsey Hill House tour 74
Ramsey Hill 79, 82, 83, 85
Ramsey Street 9, 92
Ramsey Hill Association 80
Red Carpet Sauna 89, 137, 199
Red Balloon Book Store 146
Reserve Electric Motor Project 19
Reserve Garden Lots 21
Reserve Township 13
Restaurants 172
Rice Street 9
Rice, Henry 68
Rice, Mary 119, 120, 129, 145, 200
Rockin' Hollywoods 124
Rondo Street 57, 60
Rondo Neighborhood 58
Rondo-St. Anthony Improvement Association 62
Rosedale Pharmacy 50
Rosen, Milt 91
Rudolph, Paul 158
Rugg House 76
Rupp, John 117
Ryan, Don 161, 175
Ryan, Roger 142

Saji Ya 111
Sawyer, Harry (Dutch) 45
Scarlett, Vicenta Donnelly 37
Selby Avenue 17, 22, 29, 32, 57, 60, 85
Selby and Dale 69
Selby Avenue Riots 69
Selby, Jeremiah W. 68
Seventh Street 17
Shapiro, Harry 36
Sibley, Col. Henry 6
Skally, Bill 94, 162
Smith, Steve 102

Smolik, Don 91, 157
Snelling Avenue 14, 21, 23
Soderman, Steve 119
Solin, Jim 94, 124, 157
St. Albans Street 17, 36
St. Anthony Avenue 23, 60
St. Clair 13-14, 27
St. Paul Street Railway Co. 14-15, 19-20
St. Thomas University 21
St. Thomas Aquinas Seminary 18
St. Clair, Wesley 36
St. Paul Housing and Redevelopment Agency 80
Starbucks 181
Stinson 13, 21
Stolpestad, James 102, 183, 194, 200
Storr, J. Norman 27
Street Cars, President's Conference 55
Street car electric 54
Street Car opening of line 20
Stringer, Philip 30
Subway Shop 192
Summit Avenue 9, 11, 13, 22, 49, 54, 57, 67, 75,
        78, 83, 105, 113
Summit Avenue Joseph Home 76
Summit Avenue Residential Preservation
        Association 116
Summit Avenue Rugg House 77
Summit Hill 56, 75, 79, 82
Summit Hill Association 79, 115-116, 170
Summit Hill Historic District 80
Summit Hill Mall 149, 169
Summit Park 7, 14, 197
Summit-University Urban Renewal Project 67
Swardson, Pam 104
Swardson, Roger 79, 93, 101, 119, 134, 199-200
Sweeney, Anna H. 27
Sweeney, Ann and Mary B. 28
Sweeney's Confectionery Store 28
Swendson, Carl D. 27
Swinney, Dick 130
Swinney, Pat and Dick 149
Sylvester, Bob 138

Tarrant, Karen 150
Teigen, Jane 94
Territorial Road 7
The Restoration 98
The Corner Grocery Store 34, 85, 134
Third Street 9, 17
Thomas, Clarence J. 50

Thomas family 156
Thomas Liquor 158
Thrice 119
Tiegen 147
Tilden Estate 102, 105
Tilton, Neal 28
Todd, J. Kennedy 20
Tolley 23
Towle Maple Syrup Company 23
Treacy, Mr. 36
Trolley, Horse-drawn 14-16
Twin City Rapid Transit Company 20, 54

University Avenue 23, 54
University Club 12
Uptown Theater 41, 114-115
Urban Renewal 67
Urban Ecology 71

Valento, Brian 125
Vavoulis, Mayor George 86
Victoria Crossing 169, 171
Victoria Crossing Financing 106, 109-110
Victoria Crossing South Mall 153
Victoria Crossing West Mall 100, 103
Victoria Street 19
Volstead Act 37

Wabasha Street 17
Walgreen's 32, 190
Walker, Platt 115
Wann, John 5, 13-14, 18, 186, 197
Warren, Ned 32, 51
Weaver, Russ 107, 110
Webb, Rick 149
Wedding Shoppe 200
Wengler, Bill 86, 110
Wengler, James 82, 100, 102, 106, 111, 113, 182,
        200
Western Avenue 9, 29, 68
White Lily Restaruant 32
Whyte, Daniel P. 27
Wig City Shop 97
Wilder, Alexander 77
Wilder Residence 78
Willwerscheid, Peter 94
Wilson, Mary 29, 95, 145
Winter, Ernie 94
Wolf, Lisbet 164
Women Business owners 145-155

Women's Advocates 164
Wozniac, Dede   126
Wright, William S. 5, 13, 14, 18, 186, 197
Wuollet, Jim 40, 94, 164
Wuollet's Bungalow Bakery 163

Yamamoto, Joyce 149
Yblonsky, Morris 34
Young Billie 95, 145
Yugand, Jerome 35, 85
Yugend, Rose and Isadore 34
Yugend, Sylviette 35

Zoning 131-144
Zlato! 220